Conte

About the Book

Encouragement is Nourishment

A Transformation Application

This book is about letting God move through you, living a more effective life in the Lord. Being encouraged as your relationship with Him is nourished. Being an encouragement to others as the Lord reveals more of Himself to you.

By, Sarah Kibbe

Artwork
Artwork with the poems was designed by Elissa Kobylak.

Scripture Used
All scriptures in this book are taken out of the Amplified version of the Bible unless otherwise noted.

Contact the Author
Sarah Kibbe is available to share on her book at your church group or event. Contact her by email or Facebook
Email: Skibbeuplift@aol.com
Facebook: Encouragement is Nourishment

Poem "Do You?"

Close your eyes,
Do you see Me?
Reach out, I am there.
If I touched you,
Would you feel Me?
If you hurt,
Do you know I care?
Know that I AM God,
Know that I AM Friend.
Know that I AM Daddy,
But most of all,
Know that I AM HERE.
And with Me,
There is no end.
Seek refuge in My love,
Seek comfort in My promise.
Seek the unknown, by
knowing, Seek boldness, and find safety.
You may not always understand, The plans I have for you.
But trust Me My sweet child, My plans will prosper you.

2 Timothy 1:7 For God did not give us a spirit of timidity (of cowardice, of craven and cringing and fawning fear), but [He has given us a Spirit] of power and of love and of calm and well-balanced mind and self control.

There is peace in knowing who we are in Christ and who our God is. The promises He has given us, gives us hope. The safety we have in His protection, and we are heirs as His children. We were made in the image of the Most High God. Do we really understand how unique, special and one of a kind each one of us are? That we are His most favorite, the apple of His eye, His sons and daughters. We are seated in heavenly places, we have access to the throne room of God at all times because we live in His presence we just need to learn how to continually renew our minds to this truth and dwell there.

PREFACE

"Encouragement is Nourishment"

By, Sarah Kibbe

Jeremiah 1:5 Before I formed you in the womb I knew [and] approved of you [as My chosen instrument], and before you were born I separated and set you apart, consecrating you; [and] I appointed you as a prophet to the nations.

God has a way of ministering to us, reaching into the deepest part of us and touching something that no one else knows how to touch. One night during service, I didn't realize how much I needed to hear a specific word from Him about how special I am to Him. And, during service He said this to me, (Before you were a seed, I knew your full potential). We forget that God doesn't look at our past. We're not defined by our mistakes, we're not defined by all the things that happened to us, or choices we made because we didn't know any better. But we're defined by who God says we are and the gifts He's places in us. So that we can go forward and learn from our past but not dwell in it and not be attached to it or defined by it.

I used to talk about things that happened in my childhood all the time. I used to say that I had no reason to hide it because it wasn't my fault. What I didn't know was that in a way I was using my words to keep these things alive in my life and in that I was attached to them. Once God led me and taught me about forgiveness, I gained understanding and now only share things as God leads me so that someone else will be ministered to. What I notice the most is that there is no longer that attachment to the stories but I am now attached to the testimony that God gave me from coming through them. A lot of times I share with people and it feels like another person's story. It is His story I just get to experience His greatness through it.

When we read the Word of God, He changes our perspective, when we let Him change our perspective, we allow Him to transform us. As we continue to be transformed, we begin to be more and more like Jesus. I pray that each and every person that seeks God through this book is impacted by it.

Read and meditate on one entry a week. Keep it on your heart and let God minister to you and reveal the good things He wants for you in your life. Remember, it's not about perfection, it's about love.

INTRODUCTION

SEEK first the kingdom of heaven

Be quick to LISTEN and slow to SPEAK

But be DOERS of the Word and not just HEARERS only, deceiving yourselves.

Encouragement is nourishment. A Transformation, Application.

Transformation application, be doers of the Word. Apply the Word in our lives, it works it's truth. The Word is sharper than the sharpest two edged sword. When we seek first the kingdom of heaven, we are transformed by the renewing of our minds. When we are quick to listen to what the Lord is telling us and revealing to us, then when it is time to speak, then what we will speak will be truth. We will speak the kingdom of heaven into the earth. And we can enjoy God's goodness, right here and right now. Be encouraged that God wants you to gain a fresh perspective.

This isn't just for you, but for the world to be touched by God's love. For God is love and He SO loves the world and He wants this truth revealed beyond the four walls of the church building. He wants it displayed in the world through the church body. It is time for the church to be what Jesus called it to be, His body. Each part has a job but the whole body has one goal, to love. Yes, there are different gifting's, each individual is unique and God is creative and will use each and every unique person to speak into lives. There is a reason we are all different. We all have the same call, just different ways and people to reach. We are all different. We are all special in His sight, but many don't yet know this.

Encouragement is nourishment, we need to feed the body. When the body feeds on the things of God, the Light of Christ shines brighter in our lives. We all need to continue to refuel with the truth so that what is represented, is truth. Jesus is the way, the truth, and the life. It is crucial that people come to salvation, but what we need to do is love people. This is truly what will draw people to Him. The love of Christ being demonstrated in the world will show the world the difference. Then they will taste and see that the Lord is good.

SEEK

Matthew 6:33- But seek (aim at and strive after) first of all His kingdom and His righteousness (His way of doing and being right), and then all these things taken together will be given you besides.

In each week there is a topic. It will always begin with a scripture. It will then be followed by a word that the Lord had given me. These are there to encourage you and minister to you. Then there is the first Heading which is {SEEK}. The purpose of this area is to encourage you as you build your prayer life. It will begin with a scripture that you can pray and then add any other scripture(s) to it that you'd like. Put yours and others names in these prayers as you find necessary. It is the opening of your conversation with the Lord. There will also be places for you to jot down names of others you are lifting in prayer and scriptures you are standing on. This is a very intimate time with the Lord. Don't rush through it but be sensitive to the Lord and let Him minister to you. As you pray something out, remember that then you thank God for it. In this you are turning your prayer into a statement of faith.

SPEAK

Proverbs 18:21 Death and life are in the power of the tongue, and they who indulge in it shall eat the fruit of it [for death or life].

The purpose of {SPEAK} is to encourage you to speak words of life over yourself. It is so important to change the way we speak. Our tongues are the rudders that will steer us in the direction we will go. I don't know about you, but I want to go in the direction of life. So take time all week to speak these scriptures. They also are pulled out of the scripture that you will study in {LISTEN}.

LISTEN

1 Samuel 3:10- And the Lord came and stood and called as at other times, Samuel! Samuel! Then Samuel answered, Speak, Lord, for Your servant is listening. This is a special time in your relationship with God. As you read the scriptures in this part, be slow to speak and patient to listen so that Holy Spirit can

speak to you and bring revelation knowledge and understanding into your heart.

What does God have to say about it? Joshua 1:8 This Book of the Law shall not depart out of your mouth, but you shall meditate on it day and night, that you may observe and do according to all that is written in it. For then you shall make your way prosperous, and then you shall deal wisely and have good success. This section will also help you better understand a verse (the one that you are standing on in {SPEAK}). It allows you to study the connected verses as well. This is an amazing time for clarity and revelation. I'm believing that God will show you so much from this.

HEAR

Prov. 2:2-5 Making your ear attentive to skillful and godly Wisdom and inclining and directing your heart and mind to understanding [applying all your powers to the quest for it]; Yes, if you cry out for insight and raise your voice for understanding, If you seek [Wisdom] as for silver and search for skillful and godly Wisdom as for hidden treasures, Then you will understand the reverent and worshipful fear of the Lord and find the knowledge of [our omniscient] God.

As you hear what the Lord has to say, write it down, it helps you to remember and be able to go back to it as you continue your walk with the Lord. Hear Him, learn how to recognize His voice when He speaks and how to recognize when the enemy will try to rationalize or discourage us from acknowledging and obeying God when He speaks to us.

John 10:10 The thief comes only in order to steal and kill and destroy. I came that they may have and enjoy life, and have it in abundance (to the full, till it overflows). If you aren't sure if something that came to you was from God, put it on a shelf. Keep it accessible so that when the time comes, God can and will confirm to you if it was from Him. God will communicate with us in many ways, we just have to stop limiting Him in our lives.

DO

James 1:22 But be doers of the Word [obey the message], and not merely listeners to it, betraying yourselves [into deception by reasoning contrary to the truth].

Go out there and DO IT! God giving us revelation isn't just for our own benefit, it is so that we may benefit others. You will never experience God more than when you are out there being His body as He intended.

Go out into the world. This does not always mean travel to another country, but most times it will mean, your family, your neighbors, a stranger in a store or on the street. It's more about learning how to just love everyone, and looking for opportunities to share with others what God has given you. What may seem insignificant to you, may mean the world to someone else. Stay sensitive to the Holy Spirit and be obedient to do what He prompts you to do. Know that even things that seem silly and trivial can make a huge impact to someone else in their life. God knows, we learn, He leads, we follow. Have faith and trust in the Lord in all your ways and watch what He will do.

At the end of each weekly entry you will find added sections called

BE ENCOURAGED

Closes the week with an encouraging scripture

CLARITY

Gives a brief explanation about the topic that week and

TESTIMONY

Is where I share with you ways that each topic has been a part of my life. The purpose behind these is to bring an encouraging close to the week. As you go through your week, if you have a testimony, write it down so that you can be reminded of it. Testimonies are powerful and only you, have yours.

Poem "Special to Me"

Seek Me first in every day,
Your heart hears Me,
When I say.
"Oh precious creation,
Walking with Me,
Every beauty,
I long for you to see."
Share the sunset,
Converse with Me.
Let's walk through,
A beautiful memory.
Your eyes glimmer,
With the hope I give,
It's so special to Me.
When the world tries,
To steal it away,
Remember I am always,
Here to say,
"You are one of a kind,
Special to Me.
No lie has a right
To keep you from who
I intend you to be."
I fight for you daily,
Watch over you each night.
I rejoice when your heart,
In love takes flight.
On the path that you walk.
I am right here,
Just waiting to talk.

WEEK 1 PROTECTION

Psalm 91:14-16 (Message Bible) If you'll hold on to me for dear life," says God, "I'll get you out of any trouble. I'll give you the best of care if you'll only get to know and trust me. Call me and I'll answer, be at your side in bad times; I'll rescue you, then throw you a party. I'll give you a long life, give you a long drink of salvation!"

Be at peace in your spirit. No weapon formed against you shall prosper. Your constant protection is in your Most High shelter. I will bring you through. You may be weary but My strength is sufficient. Know the reality of Me. My truth is real. My truth is forever. Your flesh falls away. Rest in Me and you will have nothing to fear. Bless others with your heart, and watch what I will do for you! If you wait on Me, I will guide your words and you will be a blessing to others. Follow My path and every step you take will have impact.

SEEK

Psalm 91 Father I praise You. I give You thanks with all my heart, because I know in my heart that because You are my Father, I dwell in Your secret place. You are the Most High God. I shall remain stable and fixed under Your shadow. I say Lord, You are my Refuge and my Fortress, my God; on You alone I lean and rely, and in You I [confidently] trust! For You deliver me from the snare of the fowler and from the deadly pestilence. You Lord cover me with Your pinions, and under Your wings I trust and find refuge; Your truth and Your faithfulness are a shield and a buckler. I shall not be afraid of the terror of the night, nor of the arrow that flies by day, nor of the pestilence that stalks in the darkness, nor of the destruction and sudden death that surprise and lay waste at noonday. A thousand may fall at my side, and ten thousand at my right hand, but it shall not come near me. Only a spectator shall I be as I witness the reward of the wicked. Because I have made You Lord my refuge, and You the Most High my dwelling place, there shall no evil befall me, nor any plague or calamity come near my tent. For You give Your angels charge over me to accompany and defend and preserve me in all my ways. They shall bear me up on their hands, lest I dash my foot against a stone. I tread upon the lion and the adder; the young lion and the serpent shall I trample underfoot. Because I have set my love upon You, therefore You deliver me; You set me on high, because I know and understand Your name. I shall call upon You, and You will be with me in trouble, You will deliver me and honor me .With long life will You satisfy me and show me Your salvation.

Continue your prayer here, keep it scriptural

_____
_____
_____
_____
_____
_____

in Jesus name, Amen (in the authority of Jesus, so be it in my life)

People you are praying for

_____
_____
_____

SPEAK

Declare this over yourself, stand on the Word of God

Psalm 91- He who dwells in the secret place of the Most High shall remain stable and fixed under the shadow of the Almighty [whose power no foe can withstand]. I will say of the Lord, He is my Refuge and my Fortress, my God; on Him I [confidently] trust! For [then] He will deliver you from the snare of the fowler and from the deadly pestilence. [Then] He will cover you with His pinions, and under His wings shall you trust and find refuge; His truth and His faithfulness are a shield and a buckler. You shall not be afraid of the terror of the night, nor of the arrow (the evil plots and slanders of the wicked) that flies by day, Nor of the pestilence that stalks in darkness, nor of the destruction and sudden death that surprise and lay waste at noonday. A thousand may fall at your side, and ten thousand at your right hand, but it shall not come near you. Only a spectator shall you be [yourself inaccessible in the secret place of the Most High] as you witness the reward of the wicked. Because you have made the Lord your refuge, and the Most High your dwelling place, there shall no evil befall you, nor any plague or calamity come near your tent. For He will give His angels [especial] charge over you to accompany and defend and preserve you in all your ways [of obedience and service]. They shall bear you up on their hands, lest you dash your foot against a stone. You shall tread upon the lion and adder; the young lion and the serpent shall you trample underfoot. Because he set his love upon Me, therefore will I deliver him; I will set him on high, because he knows and understands My name [has a personal knowledge of My mercy, love, and kindness-trusts and relies on Me, knowing I will never forsake him, no, never]. He shall call upon Me, and I will answer him; I will be with him in trouble, I will deliver him and honor him. With long life will I satisfy him and show him My salvation.

LISTEN

(read and meditate on these verses this week) Psalm 91

HEAR

What revelation, understanding, and wisdom did you gain this week?

_____

_____

_____

_____

DO

How did God move you? How did you apply it in your life? How do you see God transforming you?

_____

_____

_____

_____

_____

BE ENCOURAGED

2 Thessalonians 3:3 Yet the Lord is faithful, and He will strengthen [you] and set you on a firm foundation and guard you from the evil [one].

CLARITY

God is our protection. We understand that He is who we are to go to in times of trouble. However, we are so blessed that we have a Father who is always our protection from the seen and the unseen. If we can just learn that He isn't our fire extinguisher but our smoke detector when it comes to trouble, we would see and trust Him much differently.

TESTIMONY

Psalm 91 was one of the very first scriptures I learned how to stand on. I was still very young in the Lord. I had a dream one night about me on a ship with another person. It was all in black and white and he was talking to me about clothing and zippers and strange things. I didn't understand dreams or if it was from God or not I just knew it was vivid and I felt unsettled by it. So, the next day was my Bible study group and I was able to talk with one of my leaders about it. She told me about Psalm 91 and this chapter in the Bible opened up an entirely new understanding for me. I was able to pray this and and this scripture opened up God's heart to me. That He is more than a protector the way we think of protection in the natural, He is constantly protecting us from more than we will ever know.

YOUR PERSONAL TESTIMONY

_____
_____
_____
_____
_____
_____
_____

WEEK 2 SHARE GOD

Matthew 28:19-20- Go then and make disciples of all the nations, baptizing them into the name of the Father and of the Son and of the Holy Spirit, Teaching them to observe everything that I have commanded you, and behold, I am with you all the days (perpetually, uniformly, and on every occasion), to the [very] close and consummation of the age. Amen (so let it be).

Seek Him! Let others see Him in you! Be an open window and let your light shine! Move! The time is now ACT! Do not fear this time of preparation, the purpose is clear the answer and healing are here!

SEEK

1 Peter 4:10 Father thank You for the special gift, spiritual talent, ability that You have graciously given me, as I go into the day guide my steps to serve others. Help me to be a good steward of Your multi-faceted grace. Help me to use the diverse and varied gifts and abilities granted to me by Your unmerited favor.

Continue your prayer here, keep it scriptural

_____
_____
_____
_____
_____
_____

in Jesus name, Amen (in the authority of Jesus, so be it in my life)

People you are praying for

_____
_____
_____
_____

SPEAK

Declare this over yourself, stand on the Word of God Mark 16:15 And He said to them, Go into all the world and preach and publish openly the good news (the Gospel) to every creature [of the whole human race].

LISTEN

Read and meditate on these verses this week Mark 16:1-19 (The Resurrection)

HEAR

What revelation, understanding, and wisdom did you gain this week.

_____
_____
_____
_____

DO

How did God move you? How did you apply it in your life? How do you see God transforming you?

_____
_____
_____
_____

BE ENCOURAGED

Jeremiah 29:11- For I know the plans and thoughts that I have for you, 'says the LORD, 'plans for peace and well-being and not for disaster to give you a future and a hope.

CLARITY

God is your greatest fan. He's the one who created you. He knows every bit of potential that He placed inside of you. And all along the way, He is cheering you on. He is rooting for you. And He is telling you, you have nothing to be afraid of. GO FOR IT!

TESTIMONY

When we step out in something, many times God will only show us what He wants to. One of the times God asked me to step out in faith, it was to be a leader in a class. I thought I had it covered and before I would give a yes or no, I even took the class myself to be sure I understood it. It appeared to be a pretty simple task and so I had peace about it and said yes. Little did I know what I was truly walking into. All of a sudden, I shook I was more nervous than I think I had ever remembered being. In that time, I overcame a great fear with God guiding me through. Although I didn't feel like it at the time, God was cheering me on and never left my side.

When I was able to see past the lies I was believing and let God reveal to me how He wanted to use me in the class, I found that many times, there was a lot of discussion by others and I would sit back and pay attention to the class and to the voice of Holy Spirit. Often, I would have just a few words at the end, but they had great impact for most of the people in the class. It was so powerful and humbling for me to see God move through me like that. God continued to grow me in ministering to others and being sensitive to His voice as He still is growing me and will continue to. As we share God with others, God shares more of Himself with us. We are never left out. He is always speaking. he desires for us to let Him use us and His mouthpiece and hands and feet in the world.

YOUR PERSONAL TESTIMONY

_____

_____

_____

_____

_____

_____

_____

WEEK 3 PURPOSE

John 13:34 I give you a new commandment: that you should love one another. Just as I have loved you, so you too should love one another.

A body has many parts, each has a job, a function, a purpose. The same is true of the gifts of the Spirit. There are many varieties of gifts in the body and they all have a special purpose. But God is love and the heart of the gifts are all love. They are used to minister to the body to encourage and build up. So the body will take the gifts out into the world and use them to minister to, encourage, and build up by showing God's love through them.

SEEK

Matt. 25:34-36,40 Father God I pray that as I go into the day, that I remember that I am blessed and favored and appointed to eternal salvation. My heart is to be sensitive to Your voice and when You are hungry Lord, that I will give you food. When You are thirsty Lord, that I give You something to drink, that when You are lonely that I bring You close to me and welcome You and provide what You need in friendship. When You are naked that I will clothe You, and when You are sick that I visit You and minister to You. When You are in prison, whether in the natural or in bondage in the spiritual that I will come to see You. I will seek You in this day Lord, that I will find You in the least of all men, honoring them in knowing that as I do these things for them, I am doing these things to You and as this ministers to them, Lord I remember it is ministering to You. Thank You Lord that You find me usable and that You are well pleased in who You've made me to be. In Jesus name Amen

Continue your prayer here, keep it scriptural:

_____
_____
_____
_____
_____
_____

In Jesus name, Amen (in the authority of Jesus, so be it in my life)

People you are praying for:

_____

_____

_____

_____

SPEAK

Declare this over yourself, stand on the Word of God. Romans 8:28 We are assured and know that [God being a partner in their labor] all things work together and are [fitting into a plan] for good to and for those who love God and are called according to [His] design and purpose.

LISTEN

Read and meditate on these verses this week. Romans 8:18-30 (The Future Glory)

HEAR

What revelation, understanding, and wisdom did you gain this week?

_____

_____

_____

_____

_____

DO

How did God move you? How did you apply it in your life this week? How do you see God transforming you?

_____

_____

_____

_____

_____

BE ENCOURAGED

Deuteronomy 28:12 The Lord shall open to you His good treasury, the heavens, to give the rain of your land in its season and to bless all the work of your hands; and you shall lend to many nations, but you shall not borrow.

CLARITY

God's heart for you isn't that you'd ever be in debt, but that you would be a lender. That you would be able to bless others because you are so prosperous in every way, not just financial. That the overflow can pour out to others for His glory. And He will continue to pour into your life and meet all of your needs.

TESTIMONY

It is so funny how we grow in understanding when we begin to learn about things. When I began to learn about the gifts of the Spirit, I was still a baby Christian. I was so hungry for God to use me and I wanted God to give me every gift. I wanted to be used in every possible way. I simply was so hungry that I wanted to eat everything up. As I grew further in understanding, God revealed to me the truth of His gifts. Each and every one of them is precious as each and every one of us is precious. It's about not worrying about what gifts we have, but it's about being who God made us to be and be open to however He wants to use us.

The more we let go of trying to figure this out, the more we focus on God and watch Him unfold His plan for our lives and we witness God in many amazing ways. I used to wait for God to use people to confirm different gifting's in me. It's amazing, God is really good at waiting for us to stop looking where He doesn't want us focused. It's about just going where He asks us and as we go, He is faithful to show. Now I enjoy however He chooses to use me, expecting that as soon as I think I know where He's taking me, that's when He will show the next step in the great journey He has me on and it's never what I think it will be, it is always way better. No matter where He takes me or how He uses me, it always glorifies Him and shows His amazing love.

YOUR PERSONAL TESTIMONY

_____

_____

_____

22

WEEK 4 UNDERSTANDING

Matthew 4:4 But He replied, It has been written, Man shall not live and be upheld and sustained by bread alone, but by every word that comes forth from the mouth of God.

Without understanding it is easy to be led into things that can seem good and we find out they are roads to destruction. Do not follow blindly, but by faith, seek the truth. With truth, revelation and wisdom, understanding comes. Our God does not want us blind or ignorant rather He wants us aware, knowledgeable, and equipped. I AM the Bread that feeds you eternal nourishment. I AM the food that you truly crave and desire. As you desire more of My Word, I will feed you greater things. You will never lack food again, if you feed on the right things.

SEEK

Ephesians 1:17-20 Father, grant me a spirit of wisdom and revelation [insight into mysteries and secrets] in the [deep and intimate] knowledge of You, by having the eyes of my heart flooded with light, so that I can know and understand the hope which You have called me, and how rich is your glorious inheritance in the saints (His set- apart ones), and [so that I can know and understand what is the immeasurable and unlimited and surpassing greatness of Your power in and for me because I believe, as demonstrated in the working of Your mighty strength. Which Father, You exerted in Christ when You raised Him from the dead and seated Him at Your own right hand in the heavenly [places].

Continue your prayer here, keep it scriptural-

_____
_____
_____
_____
_____
_____

in Jesus name, Amen (in the authority of Jesus, so be it in my life)

People you are praying for

_____
_____
_____
_____
_____

SPEAK

Declare this over yourself, stand on the Word of God 2 Corinthians 10:4- For the weapons of our warfare are not physical [weapons of flesh and blood], but they are mighty before God for the overthrow and destruction of strongholds.

LISTEN

Read and meditate on these verses this week-
2 Corinthians 10:1-18 (Paul Defends His Authority)

HEAR

What revelation, understanding, and wisdom did you gain this week?

_____
_____
_____
_____
_____

DO

How did God move you? How did you apply it in your life this week? How do you see God transforming you?

_____
_____
_____
_____
_____

BE ENCOURAGED

Ephesians 4:12- His intention was the perfecting and the full equipping of the saints (His consecrated people), [that they should do] the work of ministering toward building up Christ's body (the church)

CLARITY

God doesn't leave us powerless. In fact we are equipped, armed, and dangerous for the Kingdom. God sends us out and because He is with us, and He is in us, and we know the Word, we know our God, and we know who we are in Him, nothing can defeat us. The enemy is powerless over the body of Christ. When we understand that everything we need is laid out for us, all we need to do is pick it up, and apply it, God is so faithful and He is always there. He always comes through and we always have the victory.

TESTIMONY

Before I gave my life to the Lord and asked Him to take over, I like most people had plenty of work to do to straighten out the mess I got really good at making all by myself. But what I grabbed hold of was that I became a new creature in Christ and that I was changed and all the old things were passed away. I was forgiven. All things were already new. I will spend the rest of my life learning what God is teaching me, but according to My God and His Word, because of what Jesus did for me, I am already seated in heavenly places. Every day is about my relationship with Him and renewing my mind so that His perfect will, the promises He's already given to me is manifest in my life more and more. Also, when it rains, I learn how to rest in Him and what the truth is behind the distraction of the storm because in truth we can ride out the waves in peace because He is on our side. As we gain wisdom and understanding, we see that life isn't so scary because this is not our eternal, heaven is.

YOUR PERSONAL TESTIMONY

_____
_____
_____
_____
_____
_____
_____
_____

WEEK 5 EXAMPLE

Deuteronomy 5:6-7 I am the Lord your God, Who brought you out of Egypt, from the house of bondage. You shall have no other gods before Me or besides Me.

God is our creator, our redeemer, our comfort, our guide, our healer, our provider, our protection, He came and sacrificed everything for us. If we put anyone, including ourselves ahead of Him, we are dishonoring Him. We are lessening all that He has done for us. If we put God ahead of everyone and everything else, we live by example for our children, spouses, friends, even strangers. We honor God by showing others how important He is. When others see this and then see the fruit of what comes from this, they begin to seek Him as well.

SEEK

1 Peter 2:21 Father, as I have been called and I understand that [it is inseparable from my vocation. For Jesus, You, also suffered for me, leaving me [Your personal] example, so that I should follow in Your footsteps.

Continue your prayer here, keep it scriptural

_____
_____
_____
_____
_____
_____
_____

in Jesus name, Amen (in the authority of Jesus, so be it in my life)

People you are praying for

_____
_____
_____
_____
_____

SPEAK

Declare this over yourself, stand on the Word of God

James 1:22 But be doers of the Word [obey the message], and not merely listeners to it, betraying yourselves [into deception by reasoning contrary to the Truth].

LISTEN

Read and meditate on these verses this week James 1:19-27 (Listening and Doing)

HEAR

What revelation, understanding, and wisdom did you gain this week?

_____
_____
_____
_____
_____

DO

How did God move you? How did you apply it in your life this week? How do you see God transforming you?

_____
_____
_____
_____
_____

BE ENCOURAGED

John 16:33 I have told you these things, so that in Me you may have [perfect] peace and confidence. In the world you have tribulation and trials and distress and frustration; but be of good cheer [take courage; be confident, certain, undaunted]! For I have overcome the world. [I have deprived it of power to harm you and have conquered it for you.]

CLARITY

When we give permission for Jesus to be our boss, it sometimes feels like finally we have taken that final step and it's all taken care of. In the spiritual this is true. But in this world, it is only the beginning. As the body of Christ, we gave Him permission, now it is our call to be obedient. Now, He will ask things of us and as we obey, we will see His good fruit come through in our lives. Many times God will ask us to step out into something that somehow is beyond us, but that is ok because through and with Christ we can do all things. If He has asked us, it doesn't matter what it looks like, He has already done it. It is just our place to be an open and obedient vessel that He can use to pull it from the spiritual into the natural. Be a doer of the Word and watch His promises come to pass in your life and see how it draws those around you to that fruit.

TESTIMONY

When I entered into a relationship with the Lord, I only had a little understanding of who He was and what His heart was and who I was in Him and how I was supposed to live my life in Him. This in itself was so much for me to wrap my head around. But then I learned a huge lesson. God will show you one or two things at a time to work on and He won't overwhelm you, but so often it is when we do things the way He asks us to that we are often amazed by how many other things are taken care of in the process because we let God walk us through. My heart was to see everything in my life completely turn around and I was on a mission to see this happen.

But then I learned to examine myself with the Lord and to let Him work on me first. I desired peace in certain areas of mine and my family's lives and God showed me to change MY attitude. I desired certain behaviors to change, and He showed ME to be obedient. If I was butting heads with someone and we just weren't seeing eye to eye, He showed ME to examine MY heart. Hmmm, we get very good at pointing fingers because it is way easier to point out someone else's faults or blame them. But, we are the ones who walk in God's authority and power and we are the ones who shift atmospheres when we enter into something. When we let God show us, how to be an example, then we see others change around us because through obedience, blessings come.

YOUR PERSONAL TESTIMONY

_____
_____
_____
_____
_____
_____
_____
_____

WEEK 6 RECEIVE

Mark 10:52 And Jesus said to him, Go your way; your faith has healed you. And at once he received his sight and accompanied Jesus on the road.

The world will show you many things. The world will show you many things! The world will SHOW YOU many things!! But, I have brought you here for such a time as this so that you may not be conformed to this world, but be transformed by the renewing of your mind. For they can show you many things, but the world cannot show you Me. You can show Me to the world! Let your light shine, Let My love show through you. You are My body. You may have different works to do, but they are all for My perfect will. That all should come to repentance. You are My army. Rise up, be ready for each command that I give, and expect to see My glory.

SEEK

Matthew 10:8 ,Romans 2:11 Father God, I thank You that You bore the stripes that I deserved, and gave Your life that I may be made whole. I thank You Father that Your promises are a free gift for us to receive. Father, as I go into my day use me. I am called to be used by You to cure the sick, raise the dead, cleanse the lepers, and drive out demons. Freely (without pay) I have received all Your promises, freely (without charge) I will be used by You to give to others the revelation that Your promises are theirs to receive as well. For You God show no partiality [undue favor or unfairness; with You Father, one man is not different from another].

Continue your prayer here, keep it scriptural

_____
_____
_____
_____
_____
_____
_____

in Jesus name, Amen (in the authority of Jesus, so be it in my life)

31

People you are praying for

_____
_____
_____
_____
_____

SPEAK

Declare this over yourself. Stand on the Word of God. John 10:27 My sheep hear My voice, and I know them, and they follow Me.

LISTEN

Read and meditate on these verses this week John 10:22-42 (Jesus Claims to Be the Son of God)

HEAR

What revelation, understanding and wisdom did you gain this week?

_____
_____
_____
_____
_____

DO

How did God move you? How did you apply it to your week? How do you see God transforming you?

_____
_____
_____
_____
_____

BE ENCOURAGED

Jeremiah 29:11-13 For I know the thoughts and plans that I have for you, says the Lord, thoughts and plans for welfare and peace and not for evil, to give you hope in your final outcome. Then you will call upon Me, and you will come and pray to Me, and I will hear and heed you. Then you will seek Me, inquire for, and require Me [as a vital necessity] and find Me when you search for Me with all your heart.

CLARITY

As we learn to stay focused on what God says about our circumstances, our healing etc., we grow stronger in the authority He has given us. We learn to openly receive from Him because we understand that He has already done everything we need Him to do. Once, we have learned deeper truths about this, we can go out and share that same truth with others so that they gain understanding in this as well. God does not see some as more than others, He sees us all the same and His promises are given freely to all who choose to receive.

TESTIMONY

About a year into my walk with the Lord, I began experiencing terrible pains. After asking questions and going to the doctor at an urgent care, I found out that my gall bladder was the source of my symptoms. It was extremely painful. I then made an appointment with my regular doctor to have it further looked into, but thank You Jesus that the morning of my appointment, I had Bible study first. Low and behold, the very thing we were studying was faith and healing. I left there believing I was already healed although I still felt the pain. I got to the doctor's office and as I was waiting, the assistant called me over and told me I had no insurance.

This was strange because my husband's work supplied our insurance and it was fine. So I asked her how much the visit would be and she told me should would ask. She then asked me how much I could pay and I told her my current co-pay which was much less than the cost without it. She went back to talk with the doctor and I said, "Lord, if I'm not supposed to be here, then shut the door and I will know I don't need this because I am healed." She came back out and told me I would have to pay full price. I said thank you very much, please take me off the list, and I left. Within 5 minutes of driving home, the pain was gone and it never returned and that was about 5 years ago. I knew I had walked something out and I gained deeper understanding in how to receive from God. Now, as all this was happening, I called my husband and he informed me that someone had accidentally cancelled our insurance and it was reinstated that very day. Wow, God. There are no accidents with God. It was not His will for me to have a problem with insurance nor does God have a problem with doctors. But, He uses everything to glorify Him when we let Him. He showed me that I had a choice in that instance to rely on Him or the doctor. I spoke the words, but the understanding wasn't as deep in me as it needed to be. He let me walk it out my way for a bit, but when I was presented with a choice, I turned to Him and He was faithful and I learned so much as He walked with me through the entire situation. Now, I am able to share that testimony with others so that they may gain understanding and help them to receive what God has already given to them.

YOUR PERSONAL TESTIMONY

_____
_____
_____
_____
_____
_____
_____
_____

WEEK 7 PEACE

Psalm 46:10-11 Let be and be still, and know (recognize and understand) that I am God. I will be exalted among the nations! I will be exalted in the earth! The Lord of hosts is with us; the God of Jacob is our Refuge (our High Tower and Stronghold). Selah [pause, and calmly think of that]!

I crawl into my Daddy's lap, I know His love, I am covered by His blood and in that I overcome, because He has overcome for me. I only need be still, listen, be obedient, and know that He is my God, my Daddy, my Everything. He is my Jesus.

SEEK

Philippians 4:7-10 Father God, I thank You that Your peace [is mine that tranquil state of a soul assured of its salvation through Christ, and so fearing nothing from You and being content with its earthly lot of whatever sort that is, that peace] which transcends all understanding shall garrison and mount guard over my heart and mind in Christ Jesus.
Continue your prayer here, keep it scriptural

_____
_____
_____
_____
_____
_____
_____

In Jesus name, Amen (in the authority of Jesus, so be it in my life)

People you are praying for

_____
_____
_____
_____

SPEAK

Declare this over yourself, stand on the Word of God

John 14:27 Peace I leave with you; My [perfect] peace I give to you; not as the world gives do I give to you. Do not let your heart be troubled, nor let it be afraid. [Let My perfect peace calm you in every circumstance and give you courage and strength for every challenge.]

LISTEN

Read and Meditate on these verses this week John 14:15-31(Jesus Promises the Holy Spirit) Particularly focus on 27-31

HEAR

What revelation, understanding, and wisdom did you gain this week?_____

_____
_____
_____
_____

DO

How did God move you? How are you applying it in your life this week? How do you see God transforming you?

_____
_____
_____
_____
_____

BE ENCOURAGED

Philippians 4:6-7 Do not be anxious or worried about anything, but in everything [every circumstance and situation] by prayer and petition with thanksgiving, continue to make your [specific] requests known to God. And the peace of God [that peace which reassures the heart, that peace] which transcends all understanding, [that peace which] stands guard over your hearts and your minds in Christ Jesus [is yours].

CLARITY

Peace is a promise that God has given each of us. We have the choice to pick it up and receive it for ourselves. The love that our Father God has for us goes beyond all we could ever imagine. He is always more than enough for whatever our needs are. He is always the answer to any question. When we just rest in Him, He is always faithful to give us direction and when we seek Him first, we can rest in knowing that His way is always the best way.

TESTIMONY

When my husband had to take time off work for surgery, I really had to seek the Lord. I was about to learn a great deal about faith, obedience, and peace. I knew that in the natural, he was going to be off work for about eight weeks and that he would only get a portion of his pay. I also knew that Christmas and our youngest daughter's birthday would be at the same time as well. I knew that I would truly have to rely on God to see us through. I asked the Lord to give me direction in what to do. Instead of beginning by giving me direction, He built up my faith and encouraged me. Which is just the love of God, He is just that awesome. It was a Thursday morning and I was getting ready to go to my Bible study class. I pulled out a pair of jeans to wear that I hadn't worn in over a year. In the back pocket I found a $20 bill. It just floored me. God knew this would just pick my spirit up.

I went to class and shared with everyone what happened and we all got so excited and praised God. After class, on my way home, God put it on my heart to give the money to my husband. He helped me see that I truly needed to be lifted spiritually, but the financial blessing was for him. He needed that encouragement. He also specifically put it on my heart to tell him it was for gas. So, I did just that. I went home, gave him the money, and told him it was for gas. You would've thought I handed him a $100 dollar bill. He began smiling and asked me if I was printing $20 bills. I was amazed how God just knew what we needed that day. Later that night I was back at church for another class and I had an opportunity to get up and share with everyone the testimony of that day. As I sat down, a lady came over and handed me another $20 bill and told me she was planting a seed. Boy did she ever. All of a sudden, thoughts just started pouring in. I was to go home, find the biggest jar I had. This was to be our financial blessing jar. It was to sit on top of our refrigerator and we were to put all of our change any money that was given to us beyond our normal income and anything else that we could. We were not to touch it at all unless it was to meet a need and we had no other way to pay for it. I went home that night and shared this with my husband and he agreed to follow the plan. I put in the $20 from the lady and we both gathered our change. We continued to pour everything we could into it. The eight weeks came and went. God blessed our children with an amazing Christmas and our youngest daughter's birthday went beautifully.

By the time my husband went back to work, we never had to touch a penny and all of the money helped to pay for our oldest son to go on his first mission trip and our middle daughter to go to church camp for her first time. As we watched the money grow and our needs continue to be met, I had peace in knowing that God had already planned ahead for everything we would need and He met my expectations and more. but that is just like God. When we trust, rest in, and find peace in what he is doing, we have joy that comes through when others would be overwhelmed by the circumstance.

YOUR PERSONAL TESTIMONY

_____
_____
_____
_____
_____
_____
_____

WEEK 8 GIVE

Matthew 6:21 For where your treasure is, there will your heart be also.

You want more of God? Give more to and for God. You want to experience more of God? Live more like and for God.

SEEK

Romans 12:1-2 Father God, today I make the decisive dedication of my body [presenting all my members and faculties] as a living sacrifice, holy (devoted, consecrated) and well pleasing to You God, which is my reasonable (rational, intelligent) service and spiritual worship. Father God, I will not be conformed to this world (this age), [fashioned after and adapted to its external, superficial customs], but I will continue to be transformed (changed) by the [entire] renewal of my mind [by its new attitude], so that I may prove [for myself] what is the good and acceptable and perfect will of God, even the thing which is good and acceptable and perfect [in Your sight for me].

Continue your prayer here, keep it scriptural

_____
_____
_____
_____
_____
_____
_____
_____

In Jesus name, Amen (in the authority of Jesus, so be it in my life)

People you are praying for

_____
_____
_____
_____
_____

SPEAK

Declare this over yourself, stand on the Word of God
Luke 6:38 Give, and [gifts] will be given to you; good measure, pressed down, shaken together, and running over, will they pour into [the pouch formed by] the bosom [of your robe and used as a bag]. For with the measure you deal out [with the measure you use when you confer benefits on others], it will be measured back to you.

LISTEN

Read and meditate on these verses this week Luke 6:37-42 (Do Not Judge Others)

HEAR

What revelation, understanding, and wisdom did you gain this week?

_____
_____
_____
_____
_____

DO

How did God move you? How did you apply it in your life this week? How do you see God transforming you?

_____
_____
_____
_____
_____

BE ENCOURAGED

Romans 12:11- Never be lazy, but work hard and serve the Lord enthusiastically.

CLARITY

Enthusiastic comes from the Greek word entheos, "divinely inspired or possessed," when you look at each root, en, means in and theos means God. So, when you look at it like that, you can read the scripture this way. Never be lazy, but work hard and serve the Lord divinely inspired in God. Wow does that bring power to that scripture! God wants us to give of ourselves, that we be a living sacrifice, but He wants us to do it willingly. He also wants our hearts to be in it. We are to be inspired to do something, not just doing something because we can. God leads us in directions in that He won't just bless others, He will bless us as well.

TESTIMONY

Have you ever heard the term, you live what you learn? Well, it is very true in many ways. God can help us break things in our life that need to be, but He has to reveal these things to us. For most of my life, I had learned to be a people pleaser. It was very hard for me to say no. I would say yes to just about everything even if I had no idea how I would accomplish the task. I did this well into my 30's, but God finally began to reveal to me greater truths. We ARE to be a help, we ARE to work hard, we ARE to be involved, and we ARE to be using the gifts and talents He has placed in us. However, we also have to learn where our hearts are. Because, God wants us in a place where we are enjoying what we are doing because in that, we will be DIVINELY INSPIRED IN GOD. He will be able to bring out the potential He placed in us from the very beginning. I still have to be very prayerful of what I say yes and no to. It's not that I want to be lazy, it's that I want to be where God always intended me to be. Give, give, give and it will always be given back and we can never out give God. But, it's not about getting caught up the works of being enough but rather that we realize that in Him, we already are and it is our place to be obedient and to be willing when He does help us see our true heart's desire which will always line up with His desires.

YOUR PERSONAL TESTIMONY

_____
_____
_____
_____
_____
_____
_____

"Been Here"

I speak with a whisper
Because I am right here.
You speak with your heart,
I hear you loud and clear.
I dwell inside,
I feel it too.
I hear the words,
You need to share.
Know My sweet child,
I always care.
I hurt when you do.
I cry when you cry.
But know that My heart,
Sees the victory inside.
Speak past what you see,
Speak beyond what you know.
Speak through the fear,
Let go and let Me,
Be the voice,
That guides you through.
Know that under the sun,
There's nothing new.

WEEK 9 FORGIVENESS

Matthew 14:14 When He went ashore and saw a great throng of people, He had compassion (pity and deep sympathy) for them and cured their sick.

Matthew 18:21-23 Then Peter came up to Him and said, Lord, how many times may my brother sin against me and I forgive him and let it go? [As many as] up to seven times? Jesus answered him, I tell you, not up to seven times, but seventy times seven! Therefore the kingdom of heaven is like a human king who wished to settle accounts with his attendants.

Thankfulness can lead to repentance. Thank God for a person. They may have hurt you, but recognize the weapon the enemy intended that relationship to be. Thank God for how He turned it around and for the ways you grew from it instead. Then repent for holding un-forgiveness against that person. Forgive them, have compassion on them. Ask God to help you see them through His eyes and in that your heart will change toward them. It doesn't mean it will be a healthy relationship for you to go back to, but it means you will no longer carry un-forgiveness and God can then move you forward in the blessings He wants you to have. Un-forgiveness is a weapon formed against us. It holds us back from growing in God. It puts up walls.

SEEK

Psalm 139:23-24, Mark 11:25, Psalm 103:12 Search me [thoroughly], O God, and know my heart! Try me and know my thoughts! And see if there is any wicked or hurtful way in me, and lead me in the way everlasting. Father God, I stand in prayer today, and all things that I have been holding against, I forgive them and I am letting it drop (I am leaving it, and letting it go), Father God, I thank You that because I have chosen to forgive, You forgive me of my [own] failings and shortcomings and let them drop. Thank you Father God, that as far as the east is from the west, so far have You removed my transgressions from me.

Continue your prayer here, keep it scriptural

_____
_____
_____
_____
_____

in Jesus name, Amen (in the authority of Jesus, so be it in my life)

People you need to forgive including yourself-

_____
_____
_____
_____
_____

SPEAK

Declare this over yourself, stand on the Word of God
Ephesians 2:8- For it is by free grace (God's unmerited favor) that you are saved (delivered from judgment and made partakers of Christ's salvation) through [your] faith. And this [salvation] is not of yourselves [of your own doing, it came not through your own striving], but it is the gift of God;

LISTEN

Read and meditate on these verses this week Ephesians 2:1-10 (Made Alive With Christ)

HEAR

What revelation, understanding, and wisdom did you gain this week?

_____
_____
_____
_____
_____

DO

How did God move you? How did you apply it in your life? How do you see God transforming you?

_____

_____

_____

_____

_____

BE ENCOURAGED

Matthew 26:28-For this is My blood of the new covenant, which [ratifies the agreement and] is being poured out for many for the forgiveness of sins.

CLARITY

God always loved us first. It is because of that love that we are able to love. Jesus died on the cross for mine and your sins. So here is the perspective we need to grasp. We all needed forgiving, therefore we all need to be able to and willing to forgive. It is necessary. Un-forgiveness builds up walls, opens doors to anger and fear. Un-forgiveness can build up pride and hatred. Un-forgiveness brings separation between us and God because we are so distracted by how we feel and the offense that came at us that we are now turned away from God and walking another direction. Until we forgive and repent for our behaviors, God can do nothing in that area of our life. He wants to, but He no longer has permission to because we have taken it away and He will never go against our own free will. Don't let un-forgiveness come between you and your relationship with the Lord, there is no offense that is ever big enough to be worth it.

TESTIMONY

I had plenty of people in my past that I would have been justified in the natural to hold offense against them. I was wronged, lied about, lied to, manipulated, mistreated, judged, taken advantage of, threatened, and many other things. By multiple people. But, as I learned the power in forgiveness, those offenses no longer had the importance to me that they once did. I didn't realize that I had grown prideful because of it all and that had stopped me from pursuing God in my life. I was pursuing being right and that made me SO wrong. Thank You Jesus that I learned and got deeper revelation about why and how to forgive. That it isn't about who's right it's about not giving ground for Satan to work in my life. It's not even always about having a face to face discussion. So, I forgave, I let go and those offenses no longer have a hold on me. Now God can use what I walked through to minister to and help others who need to walk out the same thing. I went through some really hard times and some of the people who were closest to me hurt me the most, but God helped me gain perspective and I realized that it was never about me and I was only hurting myself by holding on.

YOUR PERSONAL TESTIMONY

_____

_____

_____

_____

_____

_____

_____

_____

_____

WEEK 10 HUMILITY

Luke 14:11- For everyone who exalts himself will be humbled (ranked below others who are honored or rewarded), and he who humbles himself (keeps a modest opinion of himself and behaves accordingly) will be exalted (elevated in rank).

Compared to many, I know very little. Compared to others, I may know much. In God's eyes, I know just enough for Him to teach me more. Lord, keep me mindful so I stay humble. Keep me focused on Your truth so that no weapon formed against me will have the power to condemn me. You lift me and encourage me, build me and mold me, teach me and lead me, change me and grow me. Thank you Jesus, that my walk with You will never end.

SEEK

2 Corinthians 3:5-6 Father God, it is not that I am fit (qualified and sufficient in ability) of myself to form personal judgments or to claim or count anything as coming from me, but my power and ability and sufficiency is from You God. [It is You] Who qualifies me [making me to be fit and worthy and sufficient] as a minister and dispenser of a new covenant [of salvation through Christ], not a [minister] of the letter (of legally written code) but of the Spirit; for the code [of the Law] kills, but the [Holy] Spirit makes alive.

Continue your prayer here, keep it scriptural

_____
_____
_____
_____
_____
_____
_____

in Jesus name, Amen (in the authority of Jesus, so be it in my life)

People you are praying for

_____
_____

47

_____

_____

SPEAK

Declare this over yourself, stand on the Word of God
Philippians 2:3- Do nothing from factional motives [through
contentiousness, strife, selfishness, or for unworthy ends] or
promoted by conceit and empty arrogance. Instead, in the true
spirit of humility (lowliness of mind) let each regard the others
as better than and superior to himself [thinking more highly of
one another than you do yourselves].

LISTEN

Read and meditate on these verses this week Philippians 2:1-
11 (Have the Attitude of Christ)

HEAR

What revelation, understanding, and wisdom did you gain this
week?

_____
_____
_____
_____
_____

DO

How did God move you this week? How did you apply it this
week? How do you see God transforming you?

_____
_____
_____
_____
_____

BE ENCOURAGED

James 4:6 But He gives us more grace (power of the Holy
Spirit, to meet this evil tendency and all others fully). That is
why He says, God sets Himself against the proud and

haughty, but gives grace [continually] to the lowly (those who are humbled enough to receive it).

CLARITY

In the world's way of doing things, it is completely opposite of how God does things. In the world, it's every man for himself. Do what you gotta do. Step on the little guy. Make yourself noticed and stand out in the crowd. This mentality has no humility in it. It says the only way we matter is if we obtain a certain stature. If we have so much in our bank accounts. If everyone knows our name. God wants us to lift up others. Be the one willing to do for someone else so that they may fulfill what God has for them. Be willing to be not seen and not known so that others may experience what true love is and what is truly important. When we are humble and our hearts are for God and not to be lifted into a known position or important position, that's when God can use us the most and God will be glorified in it. Don't make yourself the head. Make Jesus the Head and you will find your place and purpose. Your joy will be made full when you do.

TESTIMONY

When we are young, people ask what do we want to be when we grow up? What college do we want to go to? Where do we want to travel? So many seeds are planted in us about what we want for us. I never saw my life going in the direction it has gone, but praise God that it has. Am I rich? Not by any means. Have all my dreams come true? Not even close. Am I content? Yes. Am I happy? Yes. Am I full of joy? Yes. It's not because I have reached some goal, but I was always fighting to be a certain way so I wouldn't be vulnerable. I was always wanting to be more than what I was because I felt like a failure in so many ways. Before I even knew when God was leading me in a direction, He was. We so often see being blessed as things like a better job or more money. Sometimes when God simplifies our life or changes it, we are able to re prioritize things. I had a great job, was making the most money I ever had and I was even in the best shape I had ever been in. I was feeling pretty good about myself. I had no idea what was coming. Now, I want to make it clear. God never brings bad things into our lives, but He will allow them or through them, bring good things. It's crucial we remember that. So, as soon as my husband and I just bought a house and I had become pregnant with our third child, things were looking like we were finally going to be ok. ALL OF A SUDDEN.... the job I was at gave us two weeks notice that it was shutting down. We had to scramble and find new jobs. I found one, I made a very small fraction compared to the last one. I eventually had to quit because it was costing us for me to work there. I had no idea that God was allowing these doors to close because I needed to come to the end of myself so that when the time came, I would turn to Him. I hadn't even thought about God and church in my life at this point. But God knew that if I was doing ok on my own, I wouldn't see or understand the need for Him in my life. So, no matter where God places me, I give Him the glory when things go well, and I thank Him when I struggle, because if we are never humbled, we never have a need to rely on God.

YOUR PERSONAL TESTIMONY

_____

_____

_____

_____

_____

_____

_____

_____

WEEK 11 FAITH

Galatians 2:20 I have been crucified with Christ [in Him I have shared His crucifixion]; it is no longer I who live, but Christ (the Messiah) lives in me; and the life I live by faith in (by adherence to and reliance on and complete trust in) the Son of God, Who loved me and gave Himself up for me. My grace is sufficient, take the steps in front of you even if they don't make sense at the time. You are My child, I will not lead you astray. Follow the plan I give you, and your ark will be built with a sturdy frame. It will carry you through to your new destination where I will give you another plan and you will grow your faith and in that faith you will walk closer to Me. I am the Lord your God and I have mighty plans for you.

SEEK

Matthew 17:20, Mark 9:23 Father God, I know that I have lacked faith in areas of my life. But, I thank You Father God because I only need faith [that is living] like a grain of mustard seed, I say to this mountain Move from here to yonder place, and I thank You Father God, it is moving right now in the name of Jesus; and nothing will be impossible to me. For all things can be (are possible) to me because I believe.
(continue your prayer here, keep it scriptural)

_____
_____
_____
_____
_____
_____
_____
_____

in Jesus name, Amen (in the authority of Jesus, so be it in my life)

People you are praying for

_____
_____
_____
_____
_____

SPEAK

Declare this over yourself, stand on the Word of God

Matthew 14:28-31 And Peter answered Him, Lord, if it is You, command me to come to You on the water. He said, Come! So Peter got out of the boat and walked on the water, and he came toward Jesus. But when he perceived and felt the strong wind, he was frightened, and as he began to sink, he cried out, Lord, save me [from death]! Instantly Jesus reached out His hand and caught and held him, saying to him, O you of little faith, why did you doubt?

LISTEN

Read and meditate on these verses this week. Matthew 14: 22-36 (Jesus Walks on Water)

HEAR

What revelation, understanding, and wisdom did you gain this week?

_____
_____
_____
_____
_____

DO

How is God moving you? How did you apply it in your life this week? How do you see God transforming you?

_____
_____
_____
_____
_____

BE ENCOURAGED

Mark 11:24 For this reason I am telling you, whatever you ask for in prayer, believe (trust and be confident) that it is granted to you, and you will [get it].

CLARITY

It isn't in our perfection that God can do all things, it is because we can do all things through Christ who gives us strength. In our weakness He is glorified. By faith we take on things that in the natural are too big for us to handle on our own, but with God to lean on and rely, He helps us accomplish everything we need to.

TESTIMONY

At our church, we have a two year Bible school. I was so hungry to know God and grow in understanding. My desire had been to go to this school but I knew financially the money just wasn't there. Praise God for just the right people in our lives who know when to encourage us and how. I brought the application to a couple of women who God placed in my life and truly were spiritual Mothers to me. They encouraged me to fill out the paper work and then just trust God for the finances. So, I did just that with such excitement and an expectant heart that God was going to be good for His Word. I knew He wanted me there so I was holding Him to it. For two years, we had three semesters a year and I would need about $190.00 at the beginning of each semester. I would always come down to the week of or even the very night of class, but every semester, the cash was in hand and I was able to pay without assistance or payment plan. Boy, to stand on God's Word for two years over and over again, to trust that God had already made the way. I just needed to keep trusting, walking forward and casting down thoughts of doubt and unbelief. That truly was one of the biggest lessons in faith which grabbed hold of me and helped me understand. In the natural, I didn't have it, but I had to trust and act like I did because in the spiritual, it was already mine!

YOUR PERSONAL TESTIMONY

_____

_____

_____

_____

_____

_____

_____

WEEK 12 STAND

Galatians 5:1- In [this] freedom Christ has made us free [and completely liberated us]; stand fast then, and do not be hampered and held ensnared and submit again to a yoke of slavery [which you have once put off].

Our fight is not like the world sees a fight. It is the way we stand firm in our beliefs, the relationship we have and keep with the Lord. Every time we make a mistake or something comes up against us, it is a matter of how we handle it, who we seek in the midst of it, and what direction we choose to go.

SEEK

Ephesians 6:10-18
Father God, I thank You that I am strong in You Lord [I am empowered through my union with You]; I draw my strength from You Lord [that strength which Your boundless might provides]. Today I put on Your whole armor God [the armor of a heavy-armed soldier which You supply], that I will be able successfully to stand up against [all] the strategies and the deceits of the devil. For I am not wrestling with flesh and blood [contending only with physical opponents], but against the powers, against [the master spirits who are] the world rulers of this present darkness, against the spirit forces of wickedness in the heavenly (supernatural) sphere. Therefore I put on Your complete armor God, that I may be able to resist and stand my ground on the evil day [of danger], and, having done all [the crisis demands], to stand [firmly in my place]. I stand therefore [hold my ground], having tightened the belt of truth around my loins and having put on the breastplate of integrity and of moral rectitude and right standing with God, and having shod my feet in preparation [to face the enemy with the firm-footed stability, the promptness, and readiness produced by the good news] of the Gospel of peace. I lift up over all the [covering] shield of saving faith, upon which you can quench all the flaming missiles of the wicked [one]. And I take the helmet of salvation and the sword that the Spirit wields, which is the Word of God. I will pray at all times (on every occasion, in every season) in the Spirit, with all [manner of] prayer and entreaty. To that end I keep alert and watch with strong purpose and perseverance, interceding in behalf of all the saints (God's consecrated people).

(continue your prayer here, keep it scriptural)

_____
_____
_____
_____
_____
_____
_____
_____

in Jesus name, Amen- (in the authority of Jesus, so be it in my life)

People you are praying for

_____
_____
_____
_____
_____

SPEAK

Declare this over yourself, stand on the Word of God 1 Corinthians 16:13 Be alert and on your guard; stand firm in your faith (your conviction respecting man's relationship to God and divine things, keeping the trust and holy fervor born of faith and a part of it). Act like men and be courageous; grow in strength!

LISTEN

Read and meditate on these verses this week 1 Corinthians 16:5-18 (Paul's Final Instructions)

HEAR

What revelation, understanding, and wisdom did you gain this week?

_____
_____
_____
_____
_____

DO

How is God moving you? How did you apply it in your life this week? How do you see God transforming you?

_____
_____
_____
_____
_____

BE ENCOURAGED

Hebrews 10:23 So let us seize and hold fast and retain without wavering the hope we cherish and confess and our acknowledgement of it, for He Who promised is reliable (sure) and faithful to His word.

CLARITY

It isn't always going to be easy to stand on what God says instead of going by what we see, but the more we learn to do it, the more frequently we will see God's will and promises come to pass in our lives.

TESTIMONY

Growing up, I struggled with sinus and breathing problems. I was frequently at the doctor getting more medication for the same thing. As I learned to stand on the Word, I have learned to by faith believe in my heart, by faith say with my mouth, and by faith act according to what I was believing and speaking. Now, that being said, it doesn't mean I always become 100% better in the blink of an eye, but what used to take me three weeks and lots of medication to get over, became a few days and maybe a couple doses if things got really bad. But, every time I would not and I still do not believe or give into the way things look.

Rather, I speak the Word and sing praises and simply thank God for my healing that I know is already mine. I take authority over the attack, I thank God that I have the peace that surpasses all understanding. I ask the Lord to show me what I need to do, I do it and then I go about my day as if I were not experiencing symptoms. I also use wisdom and know that I need to get a little extra rest as well. But as I have learned to stand and not be moved and to keep standing every time the symptoms try to steal my days from me, it gets to be less and I see the victory sooner and the symptoms continue to become less each time. Thank You Jesus.

YOUR PERSONAL TESTIMONY

_____
_____
_____
_____
_____
_____
_____
_____

WEEK 13- TRANSFORM

Ephesians 4:13-15 [That it might develop] until we all attain oneness in the comprehension of the [full and accurate] knowledge of the Son of God, that [we might arrive] at really mature manhood (the completeness of personality which is nothing less than the standard height of Christ's own perfection), the measure of the fullness of the Christ and the completeness found in Him. 14 So then, we may no longer be children, tossed [like ships] to and fro between chance gusts of teaching and wavering with every changing wind of doctrine, [the prey of] the cunning and cleverness of unscrupulous men, [gamblers engaged] in every shifting form of trickery in inventing errors to mislead. 15 Rather, let our lives lovingly express truth [in all things, speaking truly, dealing truly, living truly]. Enfolded in love, let us grow up in every way and in all things into Him Who is the Head, [even] Christ (the Messiah, the Anointed One).

God doesn't want us to regurgitate the Word, but rather to take it in, eat it, get all the nutrients it has to offer, grow from it, and take it back to Him and watch what else He will add to our understanding that will continue to transform and grow us. It is our milk, our soft veggies, our grains, fruit, and meat. When we feel we understand something in God's Word, He has a way of bringing deeper meaning out of the very same Word.

SEEK

Romans 12:2 Father God, I declare that I will not be conformed to this world (this age), [fashioned after and adapted to its external, superficial customs],but I am being transformed (changed) by the [entire] renewal of my mind [by its new ideals and its new attitude], so that I may prove [for myself] what is the good and acceptable and perfect will of God, even the thing which is good and acceptable and perfect [in Your sight for me].

(continue your prayer here, keep it scriptural)

_____

_____

_____

_____

_____

_____

_____

_____

In Jesus name, Amen (in the authority of Jesus, so be it in my life)

People you are praying for

_____

_____

_____

_____

_____

SPEAK

Declare this over yourself, stand on the Word of God 1 Corinthians 1:25- [This is] because the foolish thing [that has its source in] God is wiser than men, and the weak thing [that springs] from God is stronger than men.

LISTEN

Read and meditate on these verses this week 1 Corinthians 1:18-31 (The Wisdom of God)

HEAR

What revelation, understanding, and wisdom did you gain this week?

_____

_____

_____

_____

_____

DO

How is God moving you? How did you apply His guidance to your life this week? How do you see God transforming you?

_____

_____

_____

BE ENCOURAGED

2 Corinthians 5:17- Therefore if any person is [ingrafted] in Christ (the Messiah) he is a new creation (a new creature altogether); the old [previous moral and spiritual condition] has passed away. Behold, the fresh and new has come!

CLARITY

When we accept the salvation of the Lord as ours and allow Him to be our Lord, our spirit man has been made new. We are transformed instantly. However, it is only one part of us. Our body and mind still need work. Our body is all flesh and our soul (mind, will, and emotions) need to continually be renewed. In that renewal, we learn how to put our flesh under and we progressively see our lives transform to look more like God and the fruit in our lives becomes healthier.

TESTIMONY

I remember the day I gave my life to the Lord. I also remember the weeks that followed. God just grabbed hold of me in the spiritual sense and let me cry through some things. It just felt like a time where He was cleansing me of the emotions I had held in for so long. But then He began to show me how to handle things in my life His way. None of them were about being led by emotions or fleshly desires, but by His truth and example to walk that out regardless of what the world would say or what the world provides as an appropriate response. I began to learn about true forgiveness. I began to learn about believing for something no matter what it looked like. I began to understand peace no matter what was going on around me. I am far from perfect and I can honestly say that I don't always get it all just right. As I get better and see the changes in my life, I know that I'm being transformed more into the true image of my already transformed spirit man, the true me that only God sees.

YOUR PERSONAL TESTIMONY

WEEK 14 FOCUS

Colossians 3:2 And set your minds and keep them set on what is above (the higher things), not on the things that are on earth.

Silence all other voices. I am easy to find. I'm right here. The distractions are what make it difficult. Ask Me and I will tell you what hinders you from the clarity you desire, what drowns out My voice. See past what you see. Know beyond what the world says. Speak My Truth. Recognize the atmosphere, be sensitive and aware of what tries to stay hidden. I will reveal the truth. Greater am I Who is in you. Whether in the sun, whether in the storm, My peace remains. Stand firm. Live according to My Word, My Spirit, My example. Love according to My Word, My Spirit, My example. Believe according to My Word, My Spirit, My example.

SEEK

Psalm 1:1-3 Father God, I thank You that I am blessed (happy, fortunate, prosperous, and enviable) I strive not to be the man who walks and lives in the counsel of the ungodly [choosing not to follow their advice, their plans or purposes], nor will I stand [submissive and inactive] in the path where sinners walk, nor sit down[to relax and rest] where the scornful [and the mockers] gather. But my delight and desire are in Your law Lord, and on Your law (the precepts, the instructions, the teachings of God) I habitually meditate (ponder and study) by day and by night. And I shall be like a tree firmly planted [and tended] by the streams of water, ready to bring forth my good fruit in my season; my leaf also shall not fade or wither; and everything I do shall prosper [and come to maturity].
(Continue prayer here, keep it scriptural)

_____
_____
_____
_____
_____
_____
_____

in Jesus name, Amen (in the authority of Jesus, so be it in my life)

People you are praying for

_____
_____
_____
_____
_____

SPEAK

Declare this over yourself, stand on the Word of God. Proverbs 4:25 Let your eyes look right on [with fixed purpose], and let your gaze be straight before you.

LISTEN

Read and meditate on these verses this week. Proverbs 4 (A Father's Wise Advice)

HEAR

What revelation, understanding, and wisdom did you gain this week?

_____
_____
_____
_____
_____

DO

How is God moving you? How did you apply His guidance to your life this week? How do you see God transforming you?

_____
_____
_____
_____
_____

BE ENCOURAGED

Philippians 4:8 For the rest, brethren, whatever is true, whatever is worthy of reverence and is honorable and seemly, whatever is just, whatever is pure whatever is lovely and lovable, whatever is kind and winsome and gracious, if there is any virtue and excellence, if there is anything worthy of praise, think on and weigh and take account of these things [fix your minds on them].

CLARITY

God is always talking to us, He is always focused and right where He needs to be. We so easily get off track and begin listening to the things of this world that seem good because they feel good to us for many different reasons. Don't allow the devil to beat you up about it, just talk to God and ask Him where you need to make some changes. It could be cutting back on t.v. or learning how to manage your time better. There are so many things that can cause us to be distracted, but just keep allowing God to give you a check up and write you the exact prescription you need to be focused again.

TESTIMONY

All of my life, I grew up learning to be a 'people pleaser'. Does that sound like you? I never knew how to say no and always found myself meeting everyone's needs because they asked and I didn't want to let them down. I also loved the praise that came from it. However, the more I walk with the Lord, the more purpose He puts in my days, the more I have to learn to say no. Sometimes I do really well, other times I just sit and wonder, what happened? God always gently reminds me to make Him the middle of my plate. If I do that, then He really blends into everything else in my life eventually, and then if I'm allowing Him into all areas, then He can show me things more easily because I'm seeking Him. Many times He will allow things for a season even if it isn't His best, but He will use it all for His glory one way or another.

So, I wear many hats in my life and God is slowly and gently pulling excess hats out of my life all together and teaching me through the other ones. Some will stay forever, some I'm just borrowing and some were slipped in there and need to GO. In my life I have my husband, children which I home school, extended family, my church family, my job, my areas of ministry that I am a part of. I have a heart for people and find myself pouring into others lives in any way I am able, and then the unexpected things of the every day unknown that occur. What God has shown me is that in every area of my life, there needs to be healthy and appropriate boundaries. Notice, when I listed all the hats in my life the one I left out was the hat of ME. That is where I often lose focus. When I'm so focused on everyone else, I don't set aside time for me. When I don't focus on me, I am not seeking God the way I should be. Even the good things that God has called us to do can distract us from God because we haven't sought Him about what the boundaries should be in them. Home schooling has taught me more about this than anything else. When you are mom and teacher to your children, you can mistake it as taking on the role of being everything to your children. When really it's simply taking on the role of being the main example in their life. Which means, show them that they are to be part of a team to get things done.

As the mother, I am FIRST, God's. My husband comes first after God. God is the Head, my husband is the head of my home which means he is head over the family. He is my top priority after God. Then come my children. Now as their mother, they are a critical hat for me to wear, but when I remember by keeping the standard in the order of importance in my life of God, husband, children, I am setting the correct example for them to follow and pray they do better in their lives. Then comes all the rest and when we stay focused on the order, we will see God do great things in our life.

YOUR PERSONAL TESTIMONY

_____
_____
_____
_____
_____
_____
_____
_____

WEEK 15 GOOD FRUIT

Ephesians 4:29 Let no foul or polluting language, nor evil word nor worthless talk [ever] come out of your mouth, but only such [speech] as is good and beneficial to the spiritual progress of others, as is fitting to the need and the occasion, that it may be a blessing and give grace (God's favor) to those who hear it.

Every word we speak is a seed planted. Is it a flower that brings joy? Is it a fruit that brings sweetness? Is it a vegetable that brings sustenance? Is it a tree that brings strength? Is it a weed that is meant to choke out the good? We must be mindful of the seeds we plant in ours and others lives. Plant a garden of beauty and purpose so that we and others can grow and thrive in Jesus name! It is for His glory!

SEEK

Mark 11:23 Father God, my faith is in You and I stand before this mountain. I say to this mountain, Be lifted up and thrown into the sea! I do not doubt in my heart but rather I believe that what I have said has taken place, it has been done for me. (Continue prayer here, keep it scriptural)

_____
_____
_____
_____
_____

in Jesus name, Amen (in the authority of Jesus, so be it in my life)

People you are praying for

_____
_____
_____

SPEAK

Declare this over yourself, stand on the Word of God
Proverbs 18:21 Death and life are in the power of the tongue, and they who indulge in it shall eat the fruit of it [for death or life].

LISTEN

Read and meditate on these verses this week Proverbs 18

HEAR

What revelation, understanding, and wisdom did you gain this week?

_____
_____
_____
_____
_____

DO

How is God moving you? How did you apply His guidance to your life this week? How do you see God transforming you?

_____
_____
_____
_____
_____

BE ENCOURAGED

Psalm 141:3 Set a guard, O Lord, before my mouth; keep watch at the door of my lips.

CLARITY

Our words are so powerful. They will steer us in the direction in which we will go. When our words speak what God says, we are speaking life and truth and that is what we will see come to fruition in our lives. If all we ever do is speak what we see or how we feel and things aren't so good, we are actually speaking death into whatever God is wanting for us. His will in our lives is always for life but we have responsibility in that. We shall have what we say. That is enough for me to watch my words even if I do feel a certain way or things look a certain way. God's promises are much bigger than anything we experience in the natural.

TESTIMONY

Our home was flooded in the summer time. I had more things in my basement of value than in my upstairs. We ended up with seven feet of water in our basement. Needless to say, everything was ruined. It was beautifully finished and had a gorgeous hand built wet bar. We utilized that space for so many things and did not have the money (in the natural) to replace it all. To top things off, we had no flood insurance due to unforeseen circumstances. So, I clearly remember standing at the bottom of my steps and I had a choice. I could've sat down and wept. No one would have blamed me, it was a terrible circumstance. We had nowhere else to live if things didn't work out for us. So, instead of doing what I so badly wanted to, I said "Ok, God. I'm going to roll up my sleeves, do the work that is before me and trust You to supply the rest." WOW did God move! It was in His will to restore, bless us and meet all of our needs in abundance. Because I claimed it, stood on it and acted accordingly, He was able to bring it forth in our lives.

Now, let me share this. Because we had no money to work with, we couldn't pay a crew to come and pull everything out and wash and treat the home for us, so I just got to work. Before I knew it, my amazing church family started to show up and call and it seemed like they were just coming out of the wood work. What was really happening was that God was moving on my behalf because I spoke out, believed, and acted accordingly to His Word. Those who were obedient to the voice of the Lord, came and day after day. Not only did I get the help I needed, but we were blessed above and beyond food, clothes, money, toys, and so much more. God supernaturally restored everything. As we continue to discover loses from the flood, God continues to restore according to His promise. God is faithful and always good for His Word.

YOUR PERSONAL TESTIMONY

_____
_____
_____
_____
_____
_____
_____

"As you should be"

Hush,
Do you hear?
Silence,
He draws near.
Be still,
Are you listening?
My precious Savior
Is here.
He tells me sweet truths,
I might not otherwise hear.
He holds my heart,
I know He takes great care.
He tells me truth,
He speaks strength,
Into my day.
He restores my soul,
When I hear Him say.
"I know the thoughts I think toward you,
Don't you know they are for good?
Hold onto this truth.
I know who you are,
I put it all in there,
Just as I should."
My Jesus He loves me,
He tells me sweet truths,
I might not otherwise hear.

truth AND strength

Jeremiah 29:11

WEEK 16 GRACE

Joshua 1:9 Have I not commanded you? Be strong, vigorous, and very courageous. Be not afraid, neither be dismayed, for the Lord your God is with you wherever you go.

Are you not My child? Put your faith in Me! Trust Me in all My ways. Lean not to your own understanding. For your ways are not My ways. But My grace gives you room to grow and learn. You are a new creature in Me. I Am the head and you are My body. Lay your life down for My sake and I will lift you up so that your light may shine from the highest hill and you will glorify Me. I draw the lost out of the darkness and into the light so that you may love them. I know the thoughts I think toward you. They are for good and not for disaster. To give you a hopeful end.

SEEK

Romans 12:3 Father God, thank You for Your grace (unmerited favor of God) given to me I pray that I will estimate and think of myself more highly than I ought [not to have an exaggerated opinion of my own importance], but to rate my own ability with sober judgment, each according to the degree of faith apportioned by You God to me.

Continue your prayer here, keep it scriptural

_____
_____
_____
_____
_____
_____
_____

in Jesus name, Amen (in the authority of Jesus, so be it in my life)

People you are praying for

_____
_____
_____
_____

SPEAK

Declare this over yourself, stand on the Word of God

1 peter 4:10 As each of you has received a gift (a particular spiritual talent, a gracious divine endowment), employ it for one another as [befits] good trustees of God's many-sided grace [faithful stewards of the extremely diverse powers and gifts granted to Christians by unmerited favor].

LISTEN

Read and meditate on these verses this week 1 Peter 4:1- 11 (Living For God)

HEAR

What revelation, understanding, and wisdom did you receive this week?

_____
_____
_____
_____
_____

DO

How is God moving you? How did you apply His guidance to your life this week? How do you see God transforming you?

_____
_____
_____
_____
_____

BE ENCOURAGED

Ephesians 2:8 For it is by free grace (God's unmerited favor) that you are saved (delivered from judgment and made partakers of Christ's salvation) through [your] faith. And this [salvation] is not of yourselves [of your own doing, it came not through your own striving], but it is the gift of God;

CLARITY

Nothing we could ever do or say would have ever been enough. Jesus needed to come and do for us what was impossible for man. God's unmerited favor, His grace, is so powerful that it saved all man kind and forgave us of all of our sins. It broke all of our chains and set us free. Right now, every person is free and forgiven. It's only because many are still blinded to the truth that they carry those chains. This is why God's grace also stretches into the gifts He has placed in us to go out and use them so the Truth may be brought out to those who have yet to see. It is also why the promises of God fall under His grace as well. We have already been given all of God's promises and as we learn to obtain them in the natural, the world will see the fruit in our lives and be drawn. God works all things together for the good and this truly is His best. I am not just set free so that I alone may enjoy the abundant life, but so that I may become a fisher of men and go out into the world and walk in God's grace and help others be drawn to Him that they may truly see. In my weakness, He is glorified.

TESTIMONY

In my life, I learned to be tough. Do it all myself. Carry the weight. I would have people in my life, but wouldn't allow myself to be vulnerable to them. I developed the thought that this was what strong looked like. God has since shown me what true strength is and how His grace has allowed me to grow greatly in that and He has been able to use me so much more as I open up more and soften myself more. I have learned He is my strength, my Rock, and my salvation. There was a time where I had to take care of some paperwork. There had been wall after wall put up and it needed to get done asap.

There was no more time. So, as I sat working with the person who was helping me, I quietly listened to the voice of Holy Spirit. He prompted me to offer to make a call when she couldn't find what she needed. Then as she would begin to get frustrated, I would make a light joke (appropriate of course). I was so focused on God that even when she would begin to say what everyone else had said, I would quietly speak out that I walk in the favor of God, that I would walk out with everything completed that day and this person would see the love of God in me. Low and behold, after much searching and a very small document that she wasn't even really supposed to go by, she finalized all the paperwork stood up with a smile and informed me she was going on vacation and I was her last person. I took the time to tell her how wonderful she had been and how greatly appreciated she was and I knew she didn't hear that enough. I told her God bless you and to have a safe trip. Many times we will be seed planters. I knew that day I planted a seed. God's grace was (as it always is) upon me and I have faith that He will continue to draw her and water that seed in Jesus name.

But that was nothing I did, I was simply open and obedient. In the natural I could've very easily gotten frustrated and upset, stressed her and myself out and I would've walked away with nothing and God would not have been able to plant any seeds in her life through me. I'm so thankful as I learn to walk in what God intends me to walk in that I continue to see others blessed in it. Remember, if you have been saved by grace and Jesus is your Lord and savior, His favor is on you just as much as anyone else, it's a matter of learning how to walk in it, believe in Him and dismissing the lies that would keep you from it. God is not a respecter of persons, His favor is just as strong through you as anyone else.

YOUR PERSONAL TESTIMONY

_____
_____
_____
_____
_____
_____
_____
_____
_____

Joshua 24:14-15 Now therefore [reverently] fear the Lord and serve Him in sincerity and in truth; put away the gods which your fathers served on the other side of the [Euphrates] River and in Egypt, and serve the Lord. And if it seems evil to you to serve the Lord, choose for yourselves this day whom you will serve, whether the gods which your fathers served on the other side of the River, or the gods of the Amorites, in whose land you dwell; but as for me and my house, we will serve the Lord.

You cannot force a person to drink, but lead them to the water and My love and Word will cause them to thirst after Me, My yoke is light and when they come to the end of themselves, they will drink.

SEEK

Deuteronomy 30:19 NLT Father God, today You have given me the choice between life and death, between blessings and curses. Now You call on heaven and earth to witness the choice I make. Oh, that I would choose life, so that me and my descendants might live! (Father God, I choose life and blessings this day and each day. I speak life and blessings over myself and my family and all the generations to come).

Continue your prayer here, keep it scriptural

_____
_____
_____
_____
_____
_____
_____

in Jesus name, Amen (In the authority of Jesus, so be it in my life)

People you are praying for

_____
_____
_____

SPEAK

Declare this over yourself, stand on the Word of God- Galatians 6:7-8 Do not be deceived and deluded and misled; God will not allow Himself to be sneered at (scorned, disdained, or mocked

LISTEN

Read and meditate on these verses this week Galatians 6:1-10 (We Harvest What We Plant)

HEAR

What revelation, understanding, and wisdom did you receive this week?

_____
_____
_____
_____
_____

DO

How is God moving you? How did you apply His guidance to your life this week? How do you see God transforming you?

_____
_____
_____
_____
_____

BE ENCOURAGED

Ephesians 1:4 Even as [in His love] He chose us [actually picked us out for Himself as His own] in Christ before the foundation of the world, that we should be holy (consecrated and set apart for Him) and blameless in His sight, even above reproach, before Him in love.

CLARITY

Every day is full of choices. Every day we can choose to pick up our cross and lay down our flesh. Or, just the opposite. Every day we can choose to be an example for others or we can let them influence us. Every day we can choose to be led by our emotions and focused on our circumstances, or be led by the Holy Spirit and stand on the Word of God. Every single day is full of choices. The scripture says, Choose YOU this day. We can only truly decide for ourselves, but we can be an example that shows the way to the Living Water.

TESTIMONY

As a mother, many of the testimonies I experience are with my children. This is not different. As we are a homeschooling family, we belong to co-op classes. In one of them, the parents all have responsibilities. During one of mine, I was coming down a stairway and at the very bottom, I stepped and my ankle gave out. I heard the POP and was on the floor. I Prayed immediately, stood up and slowly made my way through the rest of the day. Later that evening my dear friend came over. I was supposed to be doing something for her, but her heart was to get to me and LAY HANDS! As we were praying, my youngest Sammy was with us. Later on before bed, she approached me, laid her hands on my ankle and simply said, "By His stripes, you are healed! in Jesus name Amen!" She said it with such authority, then proceeded to ask me how my ankle was feeling. I was so filled with the joy of the Lord right then that all of me felt pretty good. She was feeling so good, she just wanted to pray over and over. So I took the time to help her understand that once you've prayed, you give thanks because it is already done. So she proceeded to give thanks and lay hands about two more times. My children see me pray all the time, but that night, God watered a seed that had been planted by example. But, she made the choice to be obedient to do it no matter how it looked to anyone else.

YOUR PERSONAL TESTIMONY

_____

_____

_____

_____

_____

WEEK 18 RIGHTEOUS

Romans 10:4 For Christ is the end of the Law [the limit at which it ceases to be, for the Law leads up to Him Who is the fulfillment of its types, and in Him the purpose which it was designed to accomplish is fulfilled. That is, the purpose of the Law is fulfilled in Him] as the means of righteousness (right relationship to God) for everyone who trusts in and adheres to and relies on Him.

I am the way, the truth, and the life. No one comes to the Father, except through Me.

His holiness and perfection are His strength, because He is pure. He does not change, His Word does not come back void and His emotions do not change with the wind. He is a just God who is true to who He is. We can always count on Him and what He says, because He does not waiver. Because of His strength we are made strong, because we are in Him, He has washed us clean, we are made righteous, He sees us as pure. Because we are His children, He is faithful and His promises remain the same and hold true forever.

SEEK

James 1:4 Father, let endurance and steadfastness and patience have full play and do a thorough work, so that I may be [a person] perfect and fully developed [with no defects],lacking in nothing.

Continue your prayer here, keep it scriptural

_____
_____
_____
_____
_____
_____
_____

in Jesus name, Amen (in the authority of Jesus, so be it in my life)

People you are praying for

_____

_____

_____

_____

_____

SPEAK

Declare this over yourself, stand on the Word of God. Isaiah 11:5 And righteousness shall be the girdle of His waist and faithfulness the girdle of His loins.

LISTEN

Read and meditate on these verses this week Isaiah 11
A Branch from David's Line

HEAR

What revelation, understanding, and wisdom did you gain this week?

_____

_____

_____

_____

_____

DO

How is God moving you? How did you apply His guidance to your life this week? How do you see God transforming you?

_____

_____

_____

_____

_____

BE ENCOURAGED

Romans 5:1 THEREFORE, SINCE we are justified (acquitted, declared righteous, and given a right standing with God) through faith, let us [grasp the fact that we] have [the peace of reconciliation to hold and to enjoy] peace with God through our Lord Jesus Christ (the Messiah, the Anointed One).

CLARITY

Righteousness is achieved only through Jesus Christ. Although, He truly makes it something we are able to acquire in our lives, it's not because of anything we can say or do. But because of everything that He is and all that He has done. Righteousness is not based on our title or stature in life but solely on who our Lord and Savior is and if we have given our lives to Him. That's it!

TESTIMONY

I grew up thinking that righteous people were priests and pastors. I also had the misunderstanding that somehow you can achieve some kind of status if you "got in good" with them. Praise the Lord, He dealt with me on that very early on. Talk about freedom. Wow, He showed me that all I needed to do was seek Him, the only truly righteous One and in Him I would be made righteous. I no longer had to work to achieve something that was impossible in my own strength, but I was able to just rest in knowing it's all about Him. Now, I trust God to bring the people He wants into my life so that He grows me the way He desires. He is a good and faithful God. Once I let go, He did some pretty amazing things. He just had to wait on me. I think He does more waiting than we do.

YOUR PERSONAL TESTIMONY-

_____
_____
_____
_____
_____
_____
_____
_____

WEEK 19 AUTHORITY

Luke 10:19 Behold! I have given you authority and power to trample upon serpents and scorpions, and [physical and mental strength and ability] over all the power that the enemy [possesses]; and nothing shall in any way harm you.

There is power in the name of Jesus. When we are children of God, we walk in the authority of Jesus, and because of that, we receive our healing, are given the strength to rise up and walk through any circumstance. Not because of anything we have done, but because of everything Jesus has done. It is worth more than all the silver and gold in the world. This is good news, this is the gift He wants everyone to receive.

SEEK

2 Corinthians 10:3-5 For though I walk (live)in the flesh, I am not carrying on my warfare according to the flesh and using mere human weapons. For the weapons of my warfare are not physical [weapons of flesh and blood], but they are mighty before God for the overthrow and destruction of strongholds, [Inasmuch as I] refute arguments and theories and reasoning's and every proud and lofty thing that sets itself up against the [true] knowledge of God; and I lead every thought and purpose away captive into the obedience of Christ (the Messiah, the Anointed One),

Continue your prayer here, keep it scriptural-

_____
_____
_____
_____
_____
_____
_____
_____

in Jesus name, Amen (in the power and authority of Jesus, so be it in my life)

People you are praying for

_____
_____
_____

SPEAK

Declare this over yourself, stand on the Word Luke 9:1 One day Jesus called together his twelve disciples and gave them power and authority to cast out all demons and to heal all diseases.

LISTEN

Read and meditate on these verses this week Luke 9:1-6 Jesus Sends Out the Twelve Disciples.

HEAR

What revelation, understanding, and wisdom did you gain this week?

_____

_____

_____

_____

_____

DO

How is God moving you? How did you apply His guidance to your life this week? How do you see God transforming you?

_____

_____

_____

_____

_____

BE ENCOURAGED

1 John 5:4-5 For whatever is born of God is victorious over the world; and this is the victory that conquers the world, even our faith. Who is that victorious over [that conquers] the world but he who believes that Jesus is the Son of God [who adheres to, trusts in, and relies on that fact]?

CLARITY

As we are children of God, we are given the right to use the name of Jesus and all the authority that is in that name. Well the name of Jesus is above every name and all things in heaven and earth and under the earth. That is a lot of power that the body of Christ does not yet know how to walk in, but we are learning and as we learn, we receive the truth and we walk in it.

TESTIMONY

A spirit of fear seems to be a very common thing to come up against. I remember when it was about a year after my home flooded that we were getting heavy rains again. One day they were putting out flood warnings and everything. Well, I had a choice, I could be afraid of my home flooding again, or I could seek God. So although my stomach tried to knot up and my brain kept telling me to start bringing things up from the basement, I began to pray. The Lord told me to go outside and start praising Him. So, I did. I walked up and down the street praying and singing praises to the Lord. Soon ,my girls were out there with me. Within about 10 minutes the rain died down to a light drizzle and it was warm so we spent then next little while playing in the water splashing and playing follow the leader. Without a care, God brought me through a literal storm. Now, I don't know if my prayer caused the rain to stop or not, but I do know that I took authority over a spirit of fear and because of that every storm after that had no effect on me. The devil saw he couldn't make me fear the rain after that because I knew the authority I walked in in that area. As we gain understanding and go boldly before the throne and use the authority that was already given to us, we see the victory manifest in our lives that is already ours that was promised and given to us from God.

YOUR PERSONAL TESTIMONY

_____

_____

_____

_____

_____

_____

_____

WEEK 20 LIVING SACRIFICE

Colossians 3:17- And whatever you do [no matter what it is] in word or deed, do everything in the name of the Lord Jesus and in [dependence upon] His Person, giving praise to God the Father through Him.

Rise up in love, walk in quiet strength. Love your enemy, use wisdom. Be quick to pay attention and slow to speak. Silence can be deafening. I am your strong tower, your Rock, your Salvation. I am the Father that covers My children. My favor is yours. The truth will always come through. Be the salt and light you were made to be. My joy is your strength. My love is your peace. Walk in truth in your day. Focus on Me, rejoice in My love for you. Don't see the circumstance, see the victory that I gave you at the cross.

SEEK

Romans 12:1-2 Father God, Today I make the decisive dedication of my body [presenting all my members and faculties] as a living sacrifice, holy (devoted, consecrated) and well pleasing to You, which is my reasonable (rational intelligent) service and spiritual worship. Father, I choose not to be conformed to this world (this age), [fashioned after and adapted to its external, superficial customs], but I am being and continue to be transformed (changed) by the [entire] renewal of my mind [by its new ideals and its new attitude], so that I may prove [for myself] what is Your good and acceptable and perfect will, even the thing which is good and acceptable and perfect [in Your sight for me].

Continue your prayer here, keep it scriptural

_____
_____
_____
_____
_____
_____
_____

in Jesus name, Amen (in the power and authority of Jesus, so be it in my life)

People you are praying for

_____
_____
_____
_____
_____

SPEAK

Declare this over yourself, stand on the Word of God-
1 Corinthians 12:13- For by [means of the personal agency of]
one [Holy] Spirit we were all, whether Jews or Greeks, slaves
or free, baptized [and by baptism united together] into one
body, and all made to drink of one [Holy] Spirit.

LISTEN

Read and meditate on these verses this week 1 Corinthians
12:12-31 One Body with Many Parts

HEAR

What revelation, understanding, and wisdom did you gain this
week?

_____
_____
_____
_____
_____

DO

How is God moving you? How did you apply His guidance to
your life this week? How do you see God transforming you?

_____
_____
_____
_____
_____

BE ENCOURAGED

Ephesians 5:1-2 Therefore be imitators of God [copy Him and
follow His example], as well-beloved children [imitate their

father]. And walk in love, [esteeming and delighting in one another] as Christ loved us and gave Himself up for us, a slain offering and sacrifice to God [for you, so that it became] a sweet fragrance.

CLARITY

As a living sacrifice, we have to continually decide to stay on or get off the altar. When faced with that choice multiple times a day, we find we slip but because Jesus was the one true sacrifice that stayed on the altar through it all, His mercy is there for us as we grow stronger and are able more and more to climb up on that altar and stay put. As we get better at walking out His example, we get better at staying put, right where we're supposed to be. We were created by the Father, who spoke us into creation by His Word. He has created us special and unique. We are filled with the gifts He has given us for a specific purpose. We are His and for Him we fulfill the purpose and plans He has for us. He is God, but we are His instruments that He uses to speak into each others lives. Even when others plot against us in some way, we are to be the salt and light. We are to live according to His way and love and pray for those even when they come against us. But the unique way He has created each of us, equips us to shift atmospheres and the truth of the matter always comes out. So, stay on course no matter what it looks like in the natural. God is always faithful.

TESTIMONY

As I was growing in hunger for the things of God, I had always found myself wondering about the baptism of the Holy Spirit. I had heard people speak in tongues, but I had very little understanding of what it truly was. Once I get to a place where I make up my mind, there's pretty much no stopping me. This can be very good and it can be very bad. Well, in this instance, it was one of the best very good times to have that mindset. So, I just decided that the opportunity came up for me to go to a short class to understand this better and then receive the baptism. I went in determined. I began to understand that it wasn't just sounds, but the perfect will of God being spoken out through me and that there was power in this baptism that I wouldn't have in my life without it. It was a part of my decision to be a living sacrifice. Because, it was an act of obedience. It was a step of faith for me because it had always been something I fought to disregard before I was walking with the Lord. I made the choice to stay put on the altar in that moment and received a very precious and powerful part of my connection and relationship with the Lord. My prayer life was completely transformed.

YOUR PERSONAL TESTIMONY

_____
_____
_____
_____
_____
_____
_____
_____
_____

"Mold-able"

My heart I open up to you,
I give it freely to all who seek.
Never underestimate,
The Words that I speak.
If only you would,
Take the time,
To ask Me what it means,
I could show you things,
Your mind could not
conceive.
For it is with the heart,
That one truly seeks.
It is through the heart,
That one truly hears,
What I speak.
Understand My Words,
Not just through what I say.
But through the heart I've
given you, Keep it mold able
as clay.

WEEK 21 RUN

1 Corinthians 9:24- Do you know that in a race all the runners compete, but [only] one receives the prize? So run [your race] that you may lay hold [of the prize] and make it yours.

I Am that I Am that I Am. I Am Your God. I Am the Lord that heals thee. I Am the Lord that lights your feet so that you may see. I have not given you a spirit of fear, so walk with the authority that I have given you. Listen for My voice. Be still and keep the peace that I have given you. Only speak the victory. See the finish line. Run your race.

SEEK

Hebrews 12:1-2 NKJV Father God, because I am surrounded by so great a cloud of witnesses, help me to lay aside every weight, and any sin which so easily tries to ensnare me, and let me run with endurance the race that is set before me, looking unto You Jesus, the author and finisher of my faith, who for the joy that was set before Him endured the cross, despising the shame, and has sat down at the right hand of the throne of God.

Continue your prayer here, keep it scriptural

_____
_____
_____
_____
_____
_____
_____

In Jesus name, Amen (in the authority of Jesus, so be it in my life)

People you are praying for-

_____
_____
_____
_____
_____

SPEAK

Declare this over yourself, stand on the Word of God. 2 Timothy 4:7- I have fought the good (worthy, honorable, and noble) fight, I have finished the race, I have kept (firmly held) the faith.

LISTEN

Read and meditate on these verses this week 2 Timothy 3:10- 2 Timothy 4:8 Paul's charge to Timothy

HEAR

What revelation, wisdom, and understanding did you gain this week?

_____
_____
_____
_____
_____

DO

How is God moving you ? How did you apply His guidance to your life this week? How do you see God transforming you?

_____
_____
_____
_____
_____

BE ENCOURAGED

Isaiah 40:31 But those who wait for the Lord [who expect, look for, and hope in Him] shall change and renew their strength and power; they shall lift their wings and mount up [close to God] as eagles [mount up to the sun]; they shall run and not be weary, they shall walk and not faint or become tired.

CLARITY

It is only as we put it all in God's hands that He can remove the weights that hold us down in our lives. It is as we trust in the Lord that He can direct our steps. He is faithful and will always show us the way when we stop carrying so much stuff around with us. If you think about a runner, what do they have with them? They wear the proper shoes. They have on the lightest clothes possible and they pace themselves. They are focused on where they are going and not where they've been. They keep their eyes and thoughts on the goal, the finish line.

TESTIMONY

I never realized all of the things I held onto when I was walking without God. Now, He was walking with me, but I KNOW I was not walking with Him. I carried all these hurts and offenses with me. Everywhere I went. When I would speak of them, I would justify them as ok because I could talk about them and not blame myself. I had been convinced that I had forgiven these people. I was so blind. However, these offenses that I had so willingly held onto kept my focus on my past and I had been deceived into believing that they were a part of me because they were a part of my past. Thank You Jesus for revelation. Once I understood what was really happening, I was able to separate my past from who I am. Now, I am moving forward into the plan and purpose, or the race God had for me to run all along. I am looking forward and only use my past as a tool to learn from and to help others learn from so that I may be a benefit to them.

For years, I let my school experience define me. I was the classic quiet girl in class. I didn't know how to be fake and when I tried to be, it never went right. I was always being teased and we never quite had the money that would help me fill the status quo at my school to be popular. I finally reached high school and just settled into being the quiet kid who only had a couple friends and that was just who I was. Boy, that is a lonely place to be in. It wasn't that a lot of friends or the right group was the problem, but the lies and the way I saw myself left me feeling very defeated and unimportant. I just had decided I wasn't anything very special. It took until I was in my thirties and gave my past to God. I found my church family, and made the decision that I was new, I had a clean slate, and I was determined to walk in that freedom that Jesus died for. I told myself I would show myself friendly to others and I prayed and asked God to surround me with the right people and for the wisdom to know who they were. He was so faithful.

Nowadays when people hear about this part of my past, they can't hardly believe it. God is always faithful and He will lighten our load so that we can run our race the best we can and succeed.

YOUR PERSONAL TESTIMONY

_____

_____

_____

_____

_____

_____

_____

_____

Ephesians 4:6 One God Father of [us] all, Who is above all [Sovereign over all], pervading all and [living] in [us] all.

Don't look at your mountain, look at Me. Don't look for the end, look for Me. Don't worry about the other side, find peace in knowing I am climbing with you. You are never alone on any path in your life, no matter what it seems like. I will make all your mountains climbable, all your oceans swim able, and all your giants beatable. You are My child and you walk in the promise I gave you at the cross. You are an over comer of ALL circumstance and are covered in My love and protection. I AM your Father your TRUE Father, I AM the one who takes every step with you, so you don't have to walk alone. So when you need Me, I will be quick to respond. I am faithful, not because you are faithful, but I am always faithful and because of that you know there is no doubt in Me. Sleep sound in the peace that I give you. Know, that when you sleep I stand watch. When you wake, I am in all that you do. When you stumble, I catch you. I lift you up when you are a babe. As you grow, I give you room. If you always believe that I am there, I will be easy to find. I will be quick to lift you, strengthen you, guide you, love you. Keep your fire for Me burning strong and I will continue to feel the heat.

SEEK

Matthew 6:26-27 Father God, as I look at the birds of the air; I see that they neither sow nor reap nor gather into barns, and yet You keep feeding them. I thank You Father, that I am worth much more than them to You. And help me Father to remember that by worrying or being anxious I cannot add one unit of measure (cubit) to my stature or to the span of my life.

Continue your prayer here, keep it scriptural

_____
_____
_____
_____
_____
_____

In Jesus name, Amen (In the authority of Jesus, so be it in my life)

People you are praying for

_____

_____

_____

_____

_____

SPEAK

Declare this over yourself, stand on the Word of God-
John 1:12-13- But to as many as did receive and welcome
Him, He gave the authority (power, privilege, right) to become
the children of God, that is, to those who believe in (adhere to,
trust in, and rely on) His name who owe their birth neither to
bloods nor to the will of the flesh [that of physical impulse] nor
to the will of man [that of a natural father], but to God. [They
are born of God!]

LISTEN

Read and meditate on these verses this week John 1:1-18
Prologue: Christ, the Eternal Word

HEAR

What revelation, wisdom and understanding did you gain this
week?

_____

_____

_____

_____

_____

DO

How is God moving you? How did you apply His guidance to
your life this week? How do you see God transforming you?

_____

_____

_____

_____

_____

BE ENCOURAGED

John 12:36- While you have the Light, believe in the Light [have faith in it, hold to it, rely on it], that you may become sons of the Light and be filled with Light. Jesus said these things, and then He went away and hid Himself from them [was lost to their view].

CLARITY

The fact remains, we live in a fallen world and things are not perfect in the natural. However, we are still children of the Most High God and we were made in His image. As we are His children, we are to reflect Him. As He is our Father, His love for us is more vast than we could ever comprehend. Because He is Father, because He is God, because He is love. We are heirs to our Father's throne. No throne is above His, and no kingdom is greater, and as His children, we are able to come boldly before His throne and stay in His presence and know that He is with us. He will never leave us nor forsake us.

TESTIMONY

In my mind I knew God was my heavenly Father, because I had been told so and had read scripture. I knew the prayer that started out with - Our Father who art in heaven. But in my heart I struggled. I wasn't familiar with the love of the Father on a personal level. I had a perception of what a father looked like and it did not line up with who God was as our Father. It took a few years. God revealed some truths to me about the difference between Him as my Father and my perceptions of a father. Then because I allowed God to walk me through some personal things, He showed me forgiveness and compassion for others. As I learned to let go of lies that had been deeply rooted in my life, I was able to make room for the love of the Father in my heart. I began to understand that He is patient, He is kind, He is not jealous or boastful or proud or rude. He does not demand His own way. He is not irritable and He keeps no record of being wronged. He rejoices when truth wins. He never gives up, never loses faith, is always hopeful and endures through every circumstance. (1 Corinthians 13 paraphrase). Because God is love, He is all these things and more. When I gained this heart understanding, I drew nearer to Him. I saw Him differently. The eyes of my heart were opened and I was forever changed. I had a fresh perspective of who He is as my Father.

YOUR PERSONAL TESTIMONY

_____
_____
_____
_____
_____
_____
_____
_____

WEEK 23 PERSPECTIVE

Luke 18:16 But Jesus called them [the parents] to Him, saying, Allow the little children to come to Me, and do not hinder them, for to such [as these] belongs the kingdom of God.

Your childlike wonder was never lost, it's just packed away. Pack away childish things, unpack your childlike wonder. God, give me the wisdom to know the difference.

SEEK

Isaiah 55:8-9 Father God, I know that Your thoughts are not my thoughts, neither are my ways Your ways, but help me to understand. Father, I know the heavens are higher than the earth, and Your ways are higher than mine and Your thoughts are higher than my thoughts. Transform me Father in thought and deed.

Continue your prayer here, keep it scriptural-

_____
_____
_____
_____
_____
_____
_____

In Jesus name, Amen (in the authority of Jesus, so be it in my life)

People you are praying for

_____
_____
_____
_____

SPEAK

Declare this over yourself, stand on the Word of God
2 Corinthians 4:18- Since we consider and look not to things that are seen but to the things that are unseen; for the things

that are visible are temporal (brief and fleeting), but the things that are invisible are deathless and everlasting.

LISTEN

Read and meditate on these verses this week 2 Corinthians 4:1-18 Treasure in Fragile Clay Jars

HEAR

What revelation, wisdom and understanding did you gain this week?

_____
_____
_____
_____
_____

DO

How is God moving you? How did you apply His guidance to your life this week? How do you see God transforming you?

_____
_____
_____
_____
_____

BE ENCOURAGED

1 Corinthians 13:11 When I was a child, I talked like a child, I thought like a child, I reasoned like a child; now that I have become a man, I am done with childish ways and have put them aside.

CLARITY

There is a big difference between being childish and being childlike. When we gain understanding, our perspective changes. We see things differently. This is one great reason why we are not equipped to judge others. Only God truly knows each of our hearts. When we behave in a childish manner, we show immaturity. We make foolish choices. We end up learning from our mistakes and having to suffer the consequences. When we open up our hearts to being childlike, we no longer put limits on God where He wants to do amazing things in us and through us. We are able to see beauty where the world sees ugly. We are able to be at peace where the world sees fear and anxiety. Having the heart of a child means having faith like a child. When we have that kind of faith, we see everything from a different perspective, we see the possibilities and answers, not the problems and worries.

TESTIMONY

When I was living according to the world, money was always a worry. I always seemed to be fighting to figure out a way to get above where I was. I would do better for a while, then it would get worse. I would sometimes fall further behind then I had been before. Now, I have learned a great deal from living on both sides of the fence so to speak. But the greatest thing I have learned is to be content with where you're at. Because things including money come and go. God is the only true constant. I began to understand and step out in faith that tithing of my finances, time, and talents and whatever else I could offer, would open doors for God to pour out blessings in my life. That doesn't mean the more I do, the more money I get. It means that as I am obedient in my heart and in my walk, God is able to manifest His promises in my life according to His Word. I am giving Him access to sustain and provide for me as I am able to have the perspective that He is good for His Word. As I do all I know to do, I will see the good fruit in my life. I am not rich by any means, but I am at peace and no longer seek a bigger bank account, but a better relationship with Him and in that I need not worry because He supplies all my needs. I also know that it is His heart for me to prosper and as I go and as I trust, good things will come both spiritual and material. The material just isn't what is important compared to Him.

YOUR PERSONAL TESTIMONY-

_____
_____
_____
_____
_____
_____
_____

WEEK 24 DISTRACTIONS

Psalm 119:15- I will meditate on Your precepts and have respect to Your ways [the paths of life marked out by Your law].

Rise up! Walk in the power I have given you. Seek My kingdom, My ways. Give, not just your money, give your time, your talents, your heart. Grow in your faith as you stand on My Word. As you gain ground in the natural, testify of Me, share My goodness with those who don't yet know. As you stay focused on Me and speak Truth over yourselves and each other, the enemy must flee. Be filled with Truth, be ye transformed. Do not be moved from your faith but move by faith. Obtain what is yours as I have promised it to you.

SEEK

Psalm 19:14 Father God, let the words of my mouth and the meditation of my heart be acceptable in Your sight, O Lord, my [firm, impenetrable] Rock and my Redeemer.

Continue your prayer here, keep it scriptural

_____
_____
_____
_____
_____

_____

In Jesus name, Amen (in the authority of Jesus, so be it in my life)

People you are praying for-

_____
_____
_____
_____
_____

SPEAK

Declare this over yourself, stand on the Word of God-
John 14:27- Peace I leave with you; My [own] peace I now give and bequeath to you. Not as the world gives do I give to

you. Do not let your hearts be troubled, neither let them be afraid. [Stop allowing yourselves to be agitated and disturbed; and do not permit yourselves to be fearful and intimidated and cowardly and unsettled.]

LISTEN

Read and meditate on these verses this week John 14:15-31 Jesus Promises the Holy Spirit

HEAR

What revelation, wisdom and understanding did you gain this week?

_____
_____
_____
_____
_____

DO

How is God moving you? How did you apply His guidance to your life this week? How do you see God transforming you?

_____
_____
_____
_____
_____

BE ENCOURAGED

James 1:12 Blessed (happy, to be envied) is the man who is patient under trial and stands up under temptation, for when he has stood the test and been approved, he will receive [the victor's] crown of life which God has promised to those who love Him.

CLARITY

When we get distracted, we loose focus. When we become distracted we are drawn off of our path. When we become distracted, there can be many reasons, but none of them are God. We become, worried or afraid. We get stressed out or too much is on our plate. We become tempted by things that used to have a hold of us. Or we want something so much that we leave God out of the picture all together and begin looking for ways to obtain it ourselves because we lack the patience to allow God to do things His way even though it is always better His way. Every day we are prone to circumstances and choices. Seek peace. If you aren't at peace, stop and take the time to find out why. Let God show you where you went off course and let Him show you how to regain your focus. Many times it's just a matter of refocusing on talking with Him. Sometimes He may show you specific things to do. Sometimes it's a matter of just backing up a few steps and letting God show you the right direction to go.

TESTIMONY

By nature, I am a doer. From circumstances, I had learned to take things into my own hands and just get things done. I learned not to rely on people because people were not reliable. God has shown me that it is ok to be a doer, but not to be an over-doer. That is a place where I find He continually has to reign me back in every so often. My eyes get big and before I know it, I have put way more on my plate than I should have. I have perfected that skill. However, I continue to get better at realizing when I do that and then let God show me what to keep on and what to take off. It gets easier to say no the more I do it. I am still a doer, but I am learning that when I do what God asks me to do, I am much more effective and it is effective for His kingdom. Just because I am capable of doing something, doesn't mean that it is what He has asked me to do. That is why prayer and focus helps so much. God wants to guide our steps, but we have to let Him. We have to learn to go to Him first and then do what He asks us to do. This is a lesson we need to continue to learn repeatedly the rest of our lives.

YOUR PERSONAL TESTIMONY-

_____
_____
_____
_____
_____
_____
_____

WEEK 25 JOY

Isaiah 40:29 He gives power to the faint and weary, and to him who has no might He increases strength [causing it to multiply and making it to abound].

Ecclesiastes 9:7 Go your way, eat your bread with joy, and drink your wine with a cheerful heart [if you are righteous, wise, and in the hands of God], for God has already accepted your works.

Let My joy abound in you. Release your faith with laughter. Dance in the storm and sing praises. Remember that I am with you in the storm.

SEEK

Romans 15:13 Father God, You are my hope. Fill me with all joy and peace in believing [through the experience of my faith] that by the power of the Holy Spirit I may abound and be overflowing (bubbling over) with hope.

Continue your prayer here, keep it scriptural

_____
_____
_____
_____
_____
_____
_____
_____

In Jesus name, Amen (in the authority of Jesus, so be it in my life)

People you are praying for

_____
_____
_____
_____
_____

SPEAK

Declare this over yourself, stand on the Word of God

Nehemiah 8:10 Then [Ezra] told them, go your way, eat the fat, drink the sweet drink, and send portions to him for whom nothing is prepared; for this day is holy to our Lord. And be not grieved and depressed, for the joy of the Lord is your strength and stronghold.

LISTEN

Read and meditate on these verses this week Nehemiah 8:1-12 Ezra reads the Law

HEAR

What revelation, wisdom, and understanding did you gain this week?

_____
_____
_____
_____
_____

DO

How is God moving you? How did you apply His guidance to your life this week? How do you see God transforming you?

_____
_____
_____
_____
_____

BE ENCOURAGED

Romans 14:17 [After all] the kingdom of God is not a matter of [getting the] food and drink [one likes], but instead it is righteousness (that state which makes a person acceptable to God) and [heart] peace and joy in the Holy Spirit.

CLARITY

The joy of the Lord is our strength. When that joy is evident in situations that most would not be able to be at peace in, or even go as far as to joke around in, this not only encourages you but it testifies of God in your life. Remember, you just never know when or how God may use you to impact someone else's life. Praise the Lord in tough times.

TESTIMONY

When I was in my late 20's, I had a job working for a person who I later found out felt very threatened by me and had a lot of troubles in their own life. However, at the time all I knew was how I was being treated. I would come home day after day crying hysterically. I began experiencing chest pains and shortness of breath which later, after an ambulance ride to the E.R. would bring to light that I was having anxiety attacks. I ended up on medication to control them and then had a second prescription to stop any that came on even while taking the medication to control them. Which, by the way, did happen. Once, even while I was driving. This went on for a few years. I felt very helpless and saw no end to it. They did eventually stop happening and praise God, I was able to stop taking the medications. A few years later, I began getting the same feeling I used to get just as they would be coming on. I locked myself in my room and began reminding the devil that I had peace that surpassed all understanding and the joy of the Lord was my strength. I had already been delivered from this and he was not going to bring it back to me. That weapon no longer had the effect Satan wanted it to. The Joy of the Lord, knowing that He would never leave me nor forsake me. He had already done everything for me that needed to be done and all I had to do was believe in my heart and say with my mouth that what I said I would have. God fills us with His unspeakable joy in so many ways. We can try to describe it in full, but there really is no way. I sat in my room and would not be moved. Made the conscious decision not to become fearful of the past affliction that used to have control in my life, Satan had no choice but to flee. As I felt the symptoms leave my body, I rejoiced and gave all the glory to God. He truly is our strength and from the strength that He gives us, we are filled with His joy.

YOUR PERSONAL TESTIMONY-

_____
_____
_____
_____
_____

WEEK 26 VULNERABLE

Galatians 5:1 In [this] freedom Christ has made us free [and completely liberated us]; stand fast then, and do not be hampered and held ensnared and submit again to a yoke of slavery [which you have once put off].

There is freedom in new levels of vulnerability. You may feel exposed, but I only remove the lies. That you would know how perfect you are in My sight. If I Am God, and I Am perfect, how could you believe that I would make anything less? You are made in My image. The only thing that keeps you from reaching the full potential of everything I made you to be, are the lies that have crept in. Let Me expose them for what they are, that together we reveal the true you that is in Me.

New levels of freedom and new levels of vulnerability.
Do not limit me, let Me take the limits off of you. I love you in the midst of the mess and into your full potential. Do not let the distractions of life keep you from focusing on Me. Distractions may scream, but I am the still small voice, the stillness and Truth overrides the noise. Do you know you are precious in My eyes? I only make beautiful. There is no other like you. Drop the chains of the lies that you carry, recognize them for what they are and know that you ARE free of them.

SEEK

Psalm 139:23-24 Father God, Search me [thoroughly], O God, and know my heart! Try me and know my thoughts! And see if there is any wicked or hurtful way in me, and lead me in the way everlasting.

Continue your prayer here, keep it scriptural

_____
_____
_____
_____
_____
_____
_____

In Jesus name, Amen (in the authority of Jesus, so be it in my life)

People you are praying for

_____
_____
_____
_____
_____

SPEAK

Declare this over yourself, Stand on the Word of God
Isaiah 61:1- The Spirit of the Lord God is upon me, because
the Lord has anointed and qualified me to preach the Gospel
of good tidings to the meek, the poor, and afflicted; He has
sent me to bind up and heal the brokenhearted, to proclaim
liberty to the [physical and spiritual] captives and the opening
of the prison and of the eyes to those who are bound,

LISTEN

Read and meditate on these verses this week Isaiah 61:1-11
Good News for the oppressed.

HEAR

What revelation, wisdom, and understanding did you gain this
week?

_____
_____
_____
_____
_____

DO

How is God moving you? How did you apply His guidance to
your life this week? How do you see God transforming?

_____
_____
_____
_____
_____

BE ENCOURAGED

Galatians 5:1 So Christ has truly set us free. Now make sure that you stay free, and don't get tied up again in slavery to the law.

CLARITY

When we are willing to be exposed to God, He is able to bring to the surface the very lies that have been keeping us in bondage. As we trust Him more, we can go to Him and allow Him to expose more in our lives. Lies need to be uprooted in our lives so that those areas can be filled with truth which will in turn produce good fruit. As we gain freedom, we can then be used to help others gain freedom in their lives as well.

TESTIMONY

The hardest thing for me to do was to admit that I had been prideful about needing the Lord in my life. When I was about 13, I had pretty much stopped going to church. My life of course had ups and downs, but the weight of it all just got heavier. People in my life began trying to talk to me about God and they would bring people to talk to me. Because of how hard my heart had gotten, I was feeling attacked instead of someone trying to encourage me. Which only pushed me further away. Then a few years later, I was in a place where God started dealing with me on some things. I didn't fully understand, but I knew enough that I was feeling drawn to go back to church. I was extremely cautious not to tell anyone except my children and husband. This had to be between me and God. The wall I had put up hadn't fully come down yet, but I was willing to be vulnerable to the Lord and listen to His voice. My children were very excited. I hadn't realized what a big deal it had been for them to go to church. This encouraged me more. I began asking people in the area. Random people who didn't know each other about any nice quiet churches in the area. Every one of them, some of which didn't even go there, all told me about the same church. So, I finally said ok God, I get it. We went to two Sunday services and that became our church family. We knew it and we didn't need to "shop around". Once, we were planted, I then began opening up and telling people where we were going and what the Lord had drawn me to. It was very freeing to leave that wall of pride in a pile of dust to blow away and never return. As I chose to be vulnerable, God walked me through and brought me to freedom and my children as well.

YOUR PERSONAL TESTIMONY

_____

_____

_____

_____

_____

_____

_____

_____

"Eyes of understanding, Heart of compassion"

Do this,
Do that,
The world tells you,
What to do.
Fear this,
Fear that,
The world tries,
To control you.
I say draw near,
Open up your heart.
If you would,
Just begin,
Your heart will,
Quickly start.
You will learn,
Just what to do,
When you see,
Someone in need.
When you look at them,
Through My eyes,
Me then, will you see.
Have compassion,
On those,
Who need what you have.
Know that I see them,
They are just as,
Precious as you.
My children deserve,
What I have to give.
Be My arms and legs,
As long as you live.

i will give you a new heart

Ezekiel 36:26

WEEK 27 COMMITMENT

1 Corinthians 11:1 Pattern yourselves after me [follow my example], as I imitate and follow Christ (the Messiah).

You are committed as I am committed to you. Wives submit to your husbands. Husbands love your wives as I love the church.

You are committed as I am committed to you. Parents, raise up your children in the way they should go.

You are committed as I am committed to you. Love one another as you love yourselves.

You are committed as I am to you. I gave it all, not for myself, but because I am committed to you, because I love you.

Give it your all every day.

As my commitment has affected your life, your commitment will affect someone else's

SEEK

Hebrews 13:21 Father God, strengthen (complete, perfect) and make me what I ought to be and equip me with everything good that I may carry out Your will; [while You Yourself] works in me and accomplishes that which is pleasing in Your sight, through Jesus Christ (the Messiah); to Whom be the glory forever and ever (to the ages of the ages. Amen (so be it).

Continue your prayer here, keep it scriptural

_____
_____
_____
_____
_____
_____
_____

in Jesus name, Amen (in the authority of Jesus, so be it in my life)

People you are praying for-

_____
_____
_____
_____
_____

SPEAK

Declare this over yourself, stand on the Word of God
 Matthew 4:19 And He said to them, Come after Me [as
disciples- letting Me be your guide], follow Me, and I will make
you fishers of men!

LISTEN

Read and meditate on these verses this week Matthew 4:18-
22 The First Disciples

HEAR

What revelation, wisdom, and understanding did you gain this
week?

_____
_____
_____
_____
_____

DO

How is God moving you? How did you apply His guidance to
your life this week? How do you see God transforming you?

_____
_____
_____
_____
_____

BE ENCOURAGED

Psalm 40:8- I delight to do your will, O my God; yes, Your law
is within my heart.

CLARITY

In committing to the Lord, it's not always easy. It's not always what we think it will be. It is never what the world's point of view is on things. God's ways are higher and when we commit to Him, we need to be willing to submit to Him. Sometimes it will be something He asks us to do and that can feel scary because it may be uncomfortable. But, so often the hardest thing He asks of us is to put our flesh under and we must learn to do it daily. Being committed to God is never about us, it's always about Him and how He wants to use us for others sake.

TESTIMONY

I was just a new born in the Lord and of course I was so excited. I was experiencing amazing things. Of course I wanted others to share in this with me. Certain people who were very close to me, I really didn't know what to do. I knew I didn't want to bombard them because I knew where that would get me. I started just quietly inviting them to church and they would turn me down. It began to wear on me. I asked the Lord for a scripture to stand on and someone came to me with the scripture Mark 6:4 which talks about a prophet being without honor in his own town and home. Although it is scripture, it didn't quite sit right with me. I asked the Lord to confirm this scripture, or to give me the one He wanted me to have. A few days later, someone else gave 1 Peter 3. Which told me how to live by example and allow the Lord to draw them through my walk. This gave me peace, direction, and hope that I could stand on. God is so faithful. I have seen so many great things come from this one powerful scripture as I made it a part of my life. Often times we forget that in committing to God, we also need to be willing to be patient and to do or not do as He wills.

YOUR PERSONAL TESTIMONY

_____
_____
_____
_____
_____
_____
_____
_____

WEEK 28 PRAISE

Psalm 86:12 I will confess and praise You, O Lord my God, with my whole (united) heart; and I will glorify Your name forevermore.

Do not fear, I am always at work. Your path is never ending. Eternity does not end, nor do My plans for you. Walk on Me (the Rock) and I will be the strength that holds you firm! What seems big to you now, is only the stepping stone to the next big thing. You are always moving on and up. Hills may seem steep sometimes but I give you the tools to climb them and the direction to do it with purpose. Praise Me as you climb and I will hear you, praise Me as you climb and the slope won't seem so steep. Praise Me when you can't see the top of that mountain, and I will show you the beauty of where you are at. Sometimes it's not about the top but it's about how you handle getting there.

SEEK

Psalm 100:4-5 Father God, I enter into Your gates with thanksgiving and a thank offering and into Your courts with praise! I am thankful and I say so to You, I bless and affectionately praise Your name! For Lord You are good; Your mercy and loving- kindness are everlasting, Your faithfulness and truth endure to all generations.

Continue your prayer here, keep it scriptural

_____
_____
_____
_____
_____
_____
_____
_____

In Jesus name, Amen (in the authority of Jesus, so be it in my life)

People you are praying for-

_____
_____
_____

_____

_____

SPEAK

Declare this over yourself, stand on the Word of God
Colossians 3:16 Let the word [spoke by] Christ (the Messiah) have its home in your hearts and minds] and dwell in you in [all its] richness, as you teach and admonish and train one another in all insight and intelligence and wisdom [in spiritual things, and as you sing] psalms and hymns and spiritual songs, making melody to God with [His] grace in your hearts.

LISTEN

Read and meditate on these verses this week Colossians 3:1-17 Living the New Life

HEAR

What revelation, wisdom, and understanding did you gain this week?

_____

_____

_____

_____

_____

DO

How is God moving you? How did you apply His guidance to your life this week? How do you see God transforming you?

_____

_____

_____

_____

_____

BE ENCOURAGED

Hebrews 13:15 Through Him, therefore, let us constantly and at all times offer up to God a sacrifice of praise, which is the fruit of lips that thankfully acknowledge and confess and glorify His name.

CLARITY

When Satan throws circumstances, obstacles, and feelings across our path. The most powerful weapon we have is our praise. It's easy to praise God when things are going well. It's even easier when He's just brought us through something. But when we praise Him in the face of the enemy in the midst of the battle, that's when we are reminded the we already have the victory. God's promises are still ours and He is still with us. The enemy may have many ways of trying to get us to pay attention to him screaming in our faces, but truly it's all one thing. The enemy comes to steal, kill, and destroy. The enemy is the father of lies and the god of this world. However, the key thing to remember is that he is defeated. He has no authority in our lives except for what we allow. Now he will try, but as we get better at remembering to praise God in the midst of it, we are able to see the victory that was already obtained for us. We go through trials, but God is always faithful and all trials end. It's how we stand in the midst of them that will make all the difference.

TESTIMONY

I have many times I can recall choosing to praise God in the midst of my trials and some more powerful testimonies than others, but I want to share one that I believe people can relate to. Now, first I want to be clear that I don't just praise God in the hard times, I try to praise Him in all times. I have three children. I home school all three and so needless to say, we have moments where there are trials. My children have learned that if things are getting a little crazy and mom starts singing praises to the Lord, it very quickly follows with , "Oh boy, mom's singing again." Well, this may seem silly to them, but it helps me keep perspective while things are not going the way I know they should be. It also helps me seek God before I handle things, so that I have an effective outcome that glorifies God, rather than an outcome that reflects how everyone is feeling. When we allow God to lead, then we get God results. When we are led by emotions, we get emotional results. So, although I am not perfect at always remembering to praise God, but oh when I do, the difference it makes. Praise God, that we can never out give Him. Even when we just give to Him our praises, He still gives back to us. What an awesome God we have.

YOUR PERSONAL TESTIMONY

_____
_____
_____
_____
_____
_____
_____
_____
_____

WEEK 29 LOVE PART 1

I'm going to ask you to slow down a little and take two weeks for this topic. It is so key that we all learn to improve our love walk with each other.

Luke 6:35-36 But love your enemies and be kind and do good [doing favors so that someone derives benefit from them] and lend, expecting and hoping for nothing in return but considering nothing as lost and despairing for no one; and then your recompense (your reward) will be great (rich, strong, intense, and abundant), and you will be sons of the Most High, for He is kind and charitable and good to the ungrateful and the selfish and wicked. So be merciful (sympathetic, tender, responsive, and compassionate even as your Father is [all these].

When you see Me, you will know Me. When you know Me, I will move you. Love can move mountains, it can move you. When you live with My love in you, you will have so much, it will need to be shared. If I am the God who created you, the God who saved you, and the God who dwells within you, then I am the God who created you to be saved so that I could dwell inside you so that you can go out into the world and show and tell others about Me, so that they can know I created them, will save them, and dwell inside them so that My love will spread and save multitudes and bring more light to a dark world. I don't move you so that you can save yourself, you are already saved. I move you so that you can move others. Be bold, even if you make mistakes, I will be pleased with you because you used your faith and that is victory that cannot be achieved any other way. The rest, let Me do, you will grow, learn, and do My will. Perfection (maturity) comes in time. Be willing to try, I will continue to teach you.

SEEK

Ephesians 4:2-3 Father God, help me to live [as becomes me] with complete lowliness of mind (humility) and meekness (unselfishness, gentleness, mildness), with patience, I pray Lord that I bear with others and make allowances because I love others. Father God, I am eager and strive earnestly to guard and keep the harmony and oneness of [and produced by] the Spirit in the binding power of peace.

Continue your prayer here, keep it scriptural

_____
_____
_____
_____
_____
_____
_____

In Jesus name, Amen (in the authority of Jesus, so be it in my life)

People you are praying for

_____
_____
_____
_____
_____

SPEAK

Declare this over yourself, stand on the Word of God-
1 John 4:7- Beloved, let us love one another, for love is (springs) from God; and he who loves [his fellowmen] is begotten (born) of God and is coming [progressively] to know and understand God [to perceive and recognize and get a better and clearer knowledge of Him].

LISTEN

Read and meditate on these verses this week 1 John 4:7-21 Loving one another

HEAR

What revelation, wisdom and understanding did you gain this week?

_____
_____
_____
_____
_____

DO

How is God moving you? How did you apply His guidance to your life this week? How do you see God transforming you?

_____

_____

_____

_____

_____

BE ENCOURAGED

1 Peter 4:8 Most important of all, continue to show deep love for each other, for love covers a multitude of sins.

CLARITY

Love is simple, but it is not easy. Love is not defined by emotions. It is defined by God, for God is love. Although He loves us, He does not make life easy for us. He walks through our trials with us, but He does not do it all for us. He has accomplished everything we need, but we must still do the work He has called us to do. We must still stand in every storm that comes our way. He will stand with us, but He won't do it all. He will never leave us, but we constantly walk away from Him in one way or another and then we have to choose to go back. But, it is because of God's love for us that we are always able to go back and He loves us even in our mistakes. Love is never easy, but it is simple. Love God, love one another, love yourself.

TESTIMONY

As I was growing up. I saw many ways that people showed emotions. I didn't understand the difference between emotion and true love. It was when I learned the scripture that tells us that God is love that I really began to seek out what that meant. Because, God is good all the time, He is a good Father, teacher, provider. The Word also tells us that obedience is better than sacrifice. We also know that there are consequences to our choices. The Word tells us that God is a gentleman and will never force us to do anything but He asks. So, I began to realize that there was so much more to TRUE love than touchy feely, googly eyes, and then eventually things go wrong and for one reason or another it ends and you move on because you got bored or tired of the other person or your feelings get hurt and so on. Then I was led to 1 Corinthians 13:4-7 this is the(NIV) version. Love is patient, love is kind. It does not envy, it does not boast, it is not proud. It does not dishonor others, it is not self-seeking, it is not easily angered, it keeps no record of wrongs. Love does not delight in evil but rejoices with truth. It always protects, always trusts, always hopes, always perseveres.

Wow was that an eye opener to me. I had learned so much about feelings and what I thought was right and wrong but it was really about why someone could be justified in how they felt, including myself in many situations. The world is led by feelings and when we are blinded from the truth, we make so many poor decisions. For me, it was a matter of looking for what I was lacking in security, compliments, provision, and much more. What I found instead was more problems, more baggage, more lack, more hurt, and less hope. I kept looking for God in all the wrong places, I just didn't know it. I didn't even realize I was looking for God. When I learned that God was all I needed, it gave me peace. That doesn't mean everything was better all of a sudden. In the spiritual it was, because I was forgiven, free, washed clean, made new. My past no longer owned me, God did because I asked Him to and He bought me with a price I could never pay myself. But in the natural, the same mess was still there and needed to be cleaned up.

Well, as we all know, we spend our lives cleaning up after ourselves because we are human and we make messes but because of God's love, He guides us, teaches us, He leads us, but He doesn't just pat us on the head and say that's ok, you keep making messes I will follow you around and clean up after you and you just keep doing whatever you want. He helps us learn how to make smaller messes, less messes and to avoid disasters. That being said, His love is so limitless that there is nothing we can do that will make Him love us any more or any less because He will never leave us nor forsake us. We have just become so accustomed to the mixed up teachings about love that we don't always know which is love and which is a mask that looks loving when it's really just feeding fleshly desires.

YOUR PERSONAL TESTIMONY

_____

_____

_____

_____

_____

_____

_____

_____

WEEK 30 LOVE PART 2

1 John 4:8 The one who does not love has not become acquainted with God [does not and never did know Him], for God is love. [He is the originator of love, and it is an enduring attribute of His nature.]

LOVE IS PATIENT Love accepts and tolerates delays, problems, or suffering without being annoyed and anxious. How many of us can honestly say we do that as we love someone. Yet, God is perfect in this. KIND- To have a good nature and disposition as a person. YUP... I'm sure we all have that one down. God, is perfect in this even when we aren't. DOES NOT ENVY- Love does not feel discontent or covet. OH yeah right none of us ever do that. But God is perfect in being content even as He looks at what is going on with all of us every single day.

DOES NOT BOAST- Love does not speak or act or carry pride. HA I'm SURE none of us get caught up in who's right or wrong EVER. But God lets us continue to be goofy and is STILL perfect in His love for us no matter how much we try to prove that we can do it our own selves as many children say when they discover independence and like it. IS NOT PROUD- Love does not show a high opinion of one's self in dignity, importance, or superiority. NOPE we never do that. But, God is perfect and came as a baby and in His life, served others no matter what position He was in. He lifted others up. DOES NOT DISHONOR- Love does not disgrace, or shame. We know where this is going but thank God that He is perfect as we all fall short. IS NOT SELF-SEEKING- Love is not selfish. RIGHT, because we never put our own wants and needs ahead of anyone else's. Thank You Jesus that You are or we would all be lost.

NOT EASILY ANGERED Love is not displeasured or belligerent or aroused by a wrong. This isn't familiar I'm sure. God is perfect in this and that He is no longer angry with us, but there is such a thing as righteous anger and when Jesus turned over the temple because of the things that were going on, He was angry. However, that doesn't mean that He just gets angry when things don't go His way, things don't go His way A LOT because we all have a tendency to go our own way on a daily basis.

KEEPS NO RECORD OF WRONGS Love forgives, it grants pardon for or remission of offense, debt, all wrong doings. It absolves. SOMETIMES we get this one down but we are far from perfect in it. God took care of that at the cross. DOES NOT DELIGHT IN EVIL BUT REJOICES WITH TRUTH- Love does not delight in things that are morally wrong or bad; immoral; wicked; harmful in any way. We struggle, but God clearly does not delight in any of these things. But God does rejoice in Truth. Love always protects, trusts, hopes, and perseveres. Love always, keeps safe from harm, relies on the integrity, strength, ability, and surety, It has confidence in. It always looks forward with great expectation. Love never gives up, pushes through even in difficulty, obstacles, and discouragement. Love is steadfast. Now, this being said, Love is not about how someone looks. It is not about how many gifts and compliments they can shower you with. Love is about who will stand with you in the storm. Who will encourage you to keep going. Who will see the beauty in you even at your ugliest because they know and love your heart. Love is simple but it is far from easy.

SEEK

James 1:4-6 Father God, I seek You that endurance may have its perfect result and do a thorough work, so that I may be perfect and completely developed [in my faith], lacking in nothing. Father, if I lack wisdom [to guide me through a decision or circumstance], I ask it of You [my benevolent] God, who gives to everyone generously and without rebuke or blame, and it will be given to me. I ask [for wisdom] in faith, without doubting [Your willingness to help], for the one who doubts is like a billowing surge of the sea that is blown about and tossed by the wind.

Continue your prayer here, keep it scriptural-

_____
_____
_____
_____
_____
_____
_____
_____

In Jesus name, Amen (in the authority of Jesus, so be it in my life)

People you are praying for

_____
_____
_____
_____
_____

SPEAK

Declare this over yourself, stand on the Word of God Luke 6:35 But love your enemies and be kind and do good [doing favors so that someone derives benefit from them] and lend, expecting and hoping for nothing in return but considering nothing as lost and despairing of no one; and then your recompense (your reward) will be great (rich, strong, intense, and abundant) and you will be sons of the Most High, for He is kind and charitable and good to the ungrateful and the selfish and wicked.

LISTEN

Read and meditate on these verses this week Luke 6:27-36 Love for Enemies

HEAR

What revelation, wisdom, and understanding did you gain this week?

_____
_____
_____
_____
_____

DO

How is God moving you? How did you apply His guidance to your life this week? How do you see God transforming you?

_____
_____
_____

BE ENCOURAGED

1 John 4:18 There is no fear in love [dread does not exist]. But perfect (complete, full-grown) love drives out fear, because fear involves [the expectation of divine] punishment, so the one who is afraid [of God's judgment] is not perfected in love [has not grown into a sufficient understanding of God's love].

CLARITY

So, remember that love is simple, but it is not easy. Sometimes quietly walking next to someone while they go through something is love because you know that if it is all done for them, they will never grow from it and get stronger. Sometimes love is meeting a need for no reason other than you have compassion for them. Love is always led with compassion it's just learning what is love and how to apply it and having your heart transformed in it that makes it a journey that continues to reveal God to us in our very own actions and reactions.

TESTIMONY

As you have learned in this book, I home school my three children. My oldest was the last to come along. I prayed and prayed and the only thing I was sure of in my heart was that I needed to wait until he was ready. I knew I could not just pull him out even if I knew it was the best thing for him. He had to come to a place where he saw it. I had to watch him walk through some very difficult things and see the effects of them. But in my heart I knew that if I just took the reins and forced what I thought on him, he would not have accepted it and I would've been fighting a loosing battle. God moves even when we aren't able to see it. Finally, after watching him go through so much, he came to me. He asked me to home school him and not to go back to school. I kept him home for a couple days, prayed and asked God for direction, clarity, and peace. He was faithful and supplied me with that and more. He never went back and although we still have the typical childhood trials, the fruit has started coming and continues to in God's way. It is a amazing journey that God has us on, even in the hard times. I am blessed to be able to be a daily part of his life to help him learn how to navigate this life with God.

YOUR PERSONAL TESTIMONY

_____
_____
_____
_____
_____
_____
_____
_____
_____

WEEK 31 PATIENCE

Revelation 3:20 Behold, I stand at the door and knock; if anyone hears and listens to and heeds My voice and opens the door, I will come in to him and will eat with him, and he [will eat] with Me.

Your steps have a purpose, My purpose. You see things unfolding, remember... things in My time, don't rush them. Be diligent and the fruit will multiply. The blessings are coming, STAY OBEDIENT. Seek Me on your path, I will reveal what you need when you need it. I will provide the light and you will know. Just trust. Just step. Be still in knowing that I will bring you through. Build others, and I will build you in it. Paths don't end, they only connect to new paths but your destination is always Me. My peace, joy, and righteousness grow in you with each step of obedience. The work is hard, but the reward is great. No man can match what I have for you. Remember, the things of this world will fall away but I remain forever. The things of this world crumble, break, and disappear. My love multiplies, grows, and will never fail you! IF, you take the time, I always have time for you. I am never too busy and will never lead you astray. Remember, you are an overcomer!

SEEK

Romans 12:12 Father God, today I rejoice and exult in hope; today I will be steadfast and patient even if there is suffering and tribulation; Father, today from beginning to end, I will be diligent in seeking You developing my prayer life that I may become constant in prayer.

Continue your prayer here, keep it scriptural-

_____
_____
_____
_____
_____
_____
_____
_____

In Jesus name, Amen (in the authority of Jesus, so be it in my life)

People you are praying for

_____
_____
_____
_____
_____

SPEAK

Declare this over yourself, stand on the Word of God Galatians 6:9 And let us not lose heart and grow weary and faint in acting nobly and doing right, for in due time and at the appointed season we shall reap, if we do not loosen and relax our courage and faint.

LISTEN

Read and meditate on these verses this week Galatians 6:1-10 We Harvest What We Plant

HEAR

What revelation, wisdom and understanding did you gain this week?

_____
_____
_____
_____
_____

DO- How is God moving you? How did you apply His guidance to your life this week? How do you see God transforming you?

_____
_____
_____
_____
_____

BE ENCOURAGED

Romans 8:25 But if we hope for what is still unseen by us, we wait for it with patience and composure.

CLARITY

We have our own time table. We as people are impatient. We as people are always wanting more, always wanting now, always wanting it fixed. We don't want to be patient and let the Lord work. We are always moving so fast and wanting to move on that we forget to let God use us right where we're at. Title and position do not define us, God does. We need to learn to stop growing weary and grow patient in the Lord. We'd be amazed at what we've been missing.

TESTIMONY

I, for as long as I can remember have been a take charge do it all kind of girl. Now, I was never so concerned about rising to the top and being some big famous high on the top of the mound kind of person, but rather I struggled with trusting that someone else would be faithful and follow through. I also have a servants heart on top of it so you can see how this can become a dangerous combo. Well, I am still a work in progress, but God has brought me far and He reigns me in more quickly now. I see it faster and I have learned to and continue to hear Him quicker and more clearly. I was always taking things on myself because I had examples in the past that showed me I had to be careful what I trusted others in. Now, there can be wisdom in knowing what someone is capable of and what is just poor judgment.

For example, I wouldn't give a 6 month old baby my bills and expect that they'd get paid, but I should be able to trust my husband to partner with me and let him make decisions too. God had to really work with me on that. I had many times been burned by trying to trust and it would blow up in my face so to speak. But as I have learned to seek God, He shows me what I should be taking on and what I should be getting rid of. In that quiet time we hear the Lord, when there is no quiet, how can we expect to hear Him? I have sought God about ministry, and I know He continues to move me in the direction He wants me to go, But as He prepares me, He uses me. Every day I have a ministry, my family, my friends, my church family, helping others when God prompts me to. Many times I will just see someone and I don't wait for them to ask, rather I ask them and you would be amazed how that will minister to a persons heart. Be content and be ready. Each day God has a plan and purpose for you. This is what I've learned, and continue to learn more and more.

YOUR PERSONAL TESTIMONY-

_____
_____
_____
_____
_____
_____
_____
_____
_____

WEEK 32 PLANTED

Ephesians 2:10 For we are God's [own] handiwork (His workmanship), recreated in Christ Jesus, [born anew] that we may do those good works which God predestined (planned beforehand) for us [taking paths which He prepared ahead of time], that we should walk in them [living the good life which He prearranged and made ready for us to live].

Do not be shallow in where I have planted your roots. Strengthen yourself by being fed and allowing your roots to grow deep. A tree does not grow strong by being uprooted and moved each day. It would wither and die. A tree is planted firmly and fed with water and sunlight that It may produce good fruit. To stand firm in your faith, you must know what you have faith in and for. I will feed you, take it in and eat. Grow and be transformed.

SEEK

Ephesians 3:14-19 Father God, may You grant out of the rich treasury of Your glory to be strengthened and reinforced with mighty power in the inner man by the [Holy] Spirit [Himself indwelling innermost being and personality]. May Christ through faith [actually] dwell (settle down, abide, make His permanent home) in heart! May be rooted deep in love and founded securely on love, That may have the power and be strong to apprehend and grasp with all the saints [God's devoted people, the experience of that love] what is the breadth and length and height and depth [of it]; [That may really come] to know [practically, through experience for yourself] the love of Christ, which far surpasses mere knowledge [without experience]; that may be filled [through all being] unto all the fullness of God [may have the richest measure of the divine Presence, and become a body wholly filled and flooded with God Himself]!

Continue your prayer here, keep it scriptural-

_____
_____
_____
_____
_____
_____

_____

_____

In Jesus name, Amen (in the authority of Jesus, so be it in my life)

People you are praying for

_____
_____
_____
_____
_____

SPEAK

Declare this over yourself, stand on the Word of God
Psalm 1:3 And he shall be like a tree firmly planted [and tended] by the streams of water, ready to bring forth its fruit in its season; its leaf also shall not fade or wither; and everything he does shall prosper [and come to maturity].

LISTEN

Read and meditate on these verses this week Psalm 1

HEAR

What revelation, wisdom and understanding did you gain this week?

_____
_____
_____
_____
_____

DO

How is God moving you? How did you apply His guidance to your life this week? How do you see God transforming you?

_____
_____
_____
_____
_____

BE ENCOURAGED

Colossians 2:7 have the roots [of your being] firmly and deeply planted [in Him, fixed and founded in Him], being continually built up in Him, becoming increasingly more confirmed and established in the faith, just as you were taught, and abounding and overflowing in it with thanksgiving.

CLARITY

As God's children He will never leave us nor forsake us. As the body of Christ, we many times struggle with staying put where He planted us to grow. A tree even as a sapling is exposed to the elements. The wind blows, the rain falls, and there are even times where water lacks. The tree is tested and tried. But, because the roots go down deep, the tree stands firm. Because the roots run deep, where the soil is still moist, the tree continues to drink. Because the roots run deep, it withstands the wind. As the body, when times get tough, when we feel offended, when life just hasn't been 'fair', that is when it matters how deep our roots go. When times get tough, you seek God, but He uses His people to be His hands and feet. When you've been offended, don't walk away and give up, good fruit never comes when the roots wither. When life hasn't been ' fair ', the body is meant to come together. It can't do that when the parts are always falling away. Don't be so quick to uproot yourself. Give it time, allow God to grow you, even when it's tough. Allow God to feed you even in the dry times. Allow God to use His whole body to work together for good. God will never leave you, but be mindful of walking away from the church family He's planted you in. He will move you when or if it is time. But there will always be good fruit when it is God.

TESTIMONY

When I was young, I got a taste of church, but I didn't go long enough and didn't have enough to get involved in to grow. I also, lived in the world for a lot longer and the only roots that grow in the world are weeds. They can grow fast and they can grow deep, but they do not strengthen or produce good fruit. They choke out and eventually kill. Be planted where God puts you. Feed on the Word and the wisdom God has given to others as He has intended wisdom for you as well. Be encouraged by those who have been there and who have been brought through by God and know from their stories that it is all ok even when it doesn't look like it. Once God planted me with my church family, I understood why it is so important to stay put. When I felt like I didn't fit or I wasn't good enough or I didn't know enough or something in my life was too big of a mess for me to belong there, I knew enough to push through the feelings and fear and in doing that, I have found perspective, wisdom, encouragement, blessings beyond what I could've hoped for and a priceless family with those who truly love me. God has blessed me with spiritual parents that have walked me through many battles, but because of God and their obedience, I have won each one. Stay where God planted you especially when it's hard you will see the fruit of it.

YOUR PERSONAL TESTIMONY

_____
_____
_____
_____
_____
_____
_____
_____

WEEK 33 DECLARE

Deuteronomy 28:13 And the Lord shall make you the head, and not the tail; and you shall be above only, and you shall not be beneath, if you heed the commandments of the Lord your God which I command you this day and are watchful to do them.

Seek rest in Me, and I will move you. I am opening doors. I am setting you up for bigger things, I am laying the foundation. I am the savior, I am the reason you have come out from under. You are the head and not the tail, you are above ONLY. Stay obedient because I am more than enough. I will bless the generations to come that seek My face. Brick by brick I build My church. I have not forsaken you. Be patient, great fruit, great signs, greatness for My glory. You are My army. Walk in obedience. You have the victory, the battle is won. You have nothing to fear. Do the work I set before you and claim the victory and the fruit will come.

SEEK

Father God, today I declare these truths over my life. I stand on your Word and I thank You that Your promises are mine because You love me more than I can comprehend. I declare that You are my God and I am Your sheep. I will follow You all the days of my life! (Psalm 100:3). I am fearfully and wonderfully made. I am special in Your sight. (Psalm 139:14). I am named after You. Thank You Jesus I am in Your family (Ephesians 3:14-15). You have given me beauty and replaced my ashes Isaiah 61:3. I am Your child I overcome because of my faith in You 1 John 5:4. Because I love you with all my heart, You Father provide everything that I need Deuteronomy 11:13-14.

Continue your declaration here, keep it scriptural

_____
_____
_____
_____
_____
_____

In Jesus name, Amen (in the authority of Jesus, so be it in my life)

People you are praying for

_____
_____
_____
_____
_____

SPEAK

Declare this over your life, stand on the Word of God John 1:12-13 But to as many as did receive and welcome Him, He gave the authority (power, privilege, right) to become the children of God, that is, to those who believe in (adhere to, trust in, and rely on) His name who owe their birth neither to bloods nor to the will of the flesh [that of physical impulse] nor to the will of man [that of a natural father], but to God. [They are born of God!]

LISTEN

Read and meditate on these verses this week John 1:1-18 Christ, the Eternal Word

HEAR

What revelation, wisdom and understanding did you gain this week?

_____
_____
_____
_____
_____

DO

How is God moving you? How did you apply His guidance to your life this week? How do you see God transforming you?

_____
_____
_____
_____
_____

BE ENCOURAGED

Luke 10:19 Behold! I have given you authority and power to trample upon serpents and scorpions, and [physical and mental strength and ability] over all the power that the enemy [possesses]; and nothing shall in any way harm you.

CLARITY

You are a child of the Most High God. None like Him and none compare. You were made in His image, you are seated with Him in heavenly places. You have authority and power. You have the right to stand and claim the promises of God and expect them to manifest in your life! Know this in your heart and speak only the Word in your every day. Get this down deep in your spirit man. Consume Truth speak Truth live Truth and know that God is always good for His Word. It's yours! Be transformed, renew your mind and speak in line with the Word and then act according to the Word before you ever see the result because in the spiritual, it is already done.

TESTIMONY

Every day I have a choice to see things the way they look in the natural or to see them according to the Word in faith. It is easy to speak what we see. It's there screaming in our faces. But, when we choose to see things not like they currently are in our lives, we see the promise more clearly and we hear the voice of the Lord more clearly and the end result is the will of God in our lives more frequently. I have walked through many tough times in my life and I have suffered many losses that no one should have to suffer. But a recent revelation that God put in my heart is this. With God, you never loose. In Him we are found. He only takes us from glory to glory to glory. He never leaves us nor forsakes us. And so on...! So I asked the Lord what does this all mean? He said to me, (I am shifting things in your life and I will be glorified in it. The end result will be for the better and mighty works I will do in the meantime. Much of what you have been declaring and thanking Me for will come to pass and you will see the glory of the Lord that you have been seeking.) This comes as we seek Him, keep our eyes on Him and wait with expectant hearts. It is our faith that moves mountains and our praise that shakes the ground. God is always on our side.

YOUR PERSONAL TESTIMONY

_____
_____
_____
_____
_____
_____
_____
_____
_____

WEEK 34 FORWARD

2 Timothy 2:15 Study and be eager and do your utmost to present yourself to God approved (tested by trial), a workman who has no cause to be ashamed, correctly analyzing and accurately dividing [rightly handling and skillfully teaching] the Word of Truth.

Seek God, if you treasure His Word, read it, do it, live it. When you focus on where you are going, you will get there. Do not let the things of this world distract you. God is faithful and if you do what He asks of you, you will see the fruit of it. He has done all He needs to and is going to do. It is your job to seek Him and submit. When you do this, you will receive what you need.

SEEK

Jeremiah 29:11-13 Father God, You know the thoughts and plans that You have for me, they are thoughts and plans for welfare and peace and not for evil, to give me hope in my final outcome. I call upon You, and I come and pray to You, and I know You hear and heed me. I seek You, inquire for, and require You [as a vital necessity] and I find You as I continue to search deeper for You with all my heart.

Continue your prayer here, keep it scriptural

_____
_____
_____
_____
_____
_____
_____

 in Jesus name, Amen (in the authority of Jesus, so be it in my life)

People you are praying for

_____
_____
_____
_____
_____

SPEAK

Declare this over yourself, stand on the Word of God James 1:22 But be doers of the Word [obey the message], and not merely listeners to it, betraying yourselves [into deception by reasoning contrary to the Truth].

LISTEN

Read and meditate on these verses this week James 1:19-26 Listening and Doing

HEAR

What revelation, wisdom, and understanding did you gain this week?

_____
_____
_____
_____
_____

DO

How is God moving you? How did you apply His guidance to your life this week? How do you see God transforming you?

_____
_____
_____
_____
_____

BE ENCOURAGED

Ezekiel 36:26-28 A new heart will I give you and a new spirit will I put within you, and I will take away the stony heart out of your flesh and give you a heart of flesh. And I will put my Spirit within you to walk in My statutes, and you shall heed My ordinances and do them. And you shall dwell in the land that I gave to your fathers; and you shall be My people and I will be your God.

CLARITY

Here is the funny thing about living for God. His way is many times simple, but so often is not easy. It is because we have to learn continually to put our flesh under and have hearts of obedience that will allow God to lead us in what we are supposed to do. It will often seem backward to us or not even make sense in the natural, but when it is done God's way, it will always move us forward and bring good fruit. It will also not just be a blessing to you, it will many times, first be a blessing to others. Because FIRST, God gave so that we may receive. As we learn more and more what this means in our lives, we will be less focused on us and our own problems and more focused on God and God kind of solutions which are truly the only solutions that heal all wounds.

TESTIMONY

I remember when I first started tithing. Boy was that a leap for me. I was one of those people that thought tithers were nuts for handing over their money to the church like that. It's one thing to throw a buck or two in but 10%?! COME ON!! But boy once God got a hold of me, I was all in. I was broke in the natural and we were barely getting by. But, then I heard a teaching in service about the widows mite. This hit my heart hard. There are so many scriptures about tithing and giving, but this one really grabbed me. I realized then, that even a few cents was giving to the kingdom the equivalent of billions because of the heart behind it. I finally chose to submit, not just in my giving but in my heart. I realized I had been robbing from the Lord without realizing the effect of what I was doing. You see, for a child of God, it is giving back to our Father what He has so abundantly blessed us with. He needs us to cooperate in works and in faith so that He can continue to do His part. If our will doesn't line up with His, He is limited by the boundaries we place on Him. So, I started giving all that I could. It started out many times in forms of change. Sometimes equaling a few dollars, sometimes less than a dollar. On the back of the envelope I would always write a scripture I was standing on for more financial blessing so that I could be a bigger blessing. The last time I remember giving change, I had a bag about the size of my hand and I placed a note inside apologizing for all the change but I was believing for a great return so I didn't have to put change in anymore.

God was so faithful. From that time on, I never put change in the tithe collection again. It was bills, it was more, and it continues to grow. I may not have millions to give, but it is more and I have seen the fruit of it. My God supplies all my needs, according to HIS riches and glory. He is a faithful God. My heart was in line with God as my giving was and because of heart obedience, He saw and was moved with compassion toward me. God is still God whether here in the flesh or in heaven. He still loves His children. When we seek God and follow His instructions, not just in deed but in our hearts, He will always move us forward.

YOUR PERSONAL TESTIMONY

_____
_____
_____
_____
_____
_____
_____
_____

WEEK 35 GOD'S WILL

1 Thessalonians 5:18- Thank [God] in everything [no matter what the circumstances may be, be thankful and give thanks], for this is the will of God for you [who are] in Christ Jesus [the Revealer and Mediator of that will].

Desire to be the reflection of Jesus, we are His body. If we do not do our part, He is limited. Not by His own doing, but by our choices. We must choose to be the arms, the feet, the back, the fingers and toes. We must choose to be whatever part of the body He has set us apart to be. We are not to seek what it is we want to be, but what it is He has called us to be. When we start just by saying "I love You Lord", "I thank You Lord", "I submit to You Lord", then we are making ourselves usable, and mold able, for Him. Once we do this, He is able to begin to shape us into the part of the body He needs us to be; So that we may be effective for Him.

SEEK

Hebrews 13:20-21 Father God, [the Author and the Giver of peace], Who brought again from among the dead our Lord Jesus, that great Shepherd of the sheep, by the blood [that sealed, ratified] the everlasting agreement (covenant, testament), Strengthen (complete, perfect) and make me what I ought to be and equip me with everything good that I may carry out Your will; [while You Yourself] works in me and accomplishes that which is pleasing in Your sight, through Jesus Christ (the Messiah); to Whom be the glory forever and ever)to the ages of the ages).

Continue your prayer here, keep it scriptural

_____
_____
_____
_____
_____
_____
_____
_____

In Jesus name, Amen (in the authority of Jesus, so be it in my life)

People you are praying for

_____
_____
_____
_____
_____

SPEAK

Declare this over yourself, stand on the Word of God-
Hebrews 10:36- For you have need of steadfast patience and endurance, so that you may perform and fully accomplish the will of God, and thus receive and carry away [and enjoy to the full] what is promised.

LISTEN

Read and meditate on these verses this week Hebrews 10:19-39 A Call to Persevere

HEAR

What revelation, wisdom and understanding did you gain this week?

_____
_____
_____
_____
_____

DO

How is God moving you? How did you apply His guidance to your life this week? How do you see God transforming you?

_____
_____
_____
_____
_____

BE ENCOURAGED

1 Timothy 2:4 Who wishes all men to be saved and [increasingly] to perceive and recognize and discern and know precisely and correctly the [divine] Truth.

CLARITY

Although we all have different gifting's, our testimonies are unique to us, and how God uses us may look different because we are all different. God's perfect will always boils down to this. That every man come to repentance and be saved. This is the perfect will of God.

TESTIMONY

So much that I never understood. So many times I tried to figure it all out on my own. How many messes I made in my life. None of this was God's will for me. I know now that He was with me through all of it. He wanted so badly to help me. He wanted so much better for me. I had to come to a place where I was ready to hear what He wanted to tell me all along. "I love you Sarah. You are my precious daughter Sarah. My body is not complete without you Sarah." And so much more. It was His will to love me and for me to love Him back. Once I came to the end of me and stopped trying to do it all alone, I saw and recognized the truth that I had been blinded from. In that love, He is able to use me more and more as I learn to love more and more. Maybe my path may look a little different than yours, but truly we are all called to the same path, LOVE.

YOUR PERSONAL TESTIMONY

_____
_____
_____
_____
_____
_____
_____
_____
_____

Luke 6:38 Give, and [gifts] will be given to you; good measure, pressed down, shaken together, and running over, will they pour into [the pouch formed by] the bosom [of your robe and used as a bag]. For with the measure you deal out [with the measure you use when you confer benefits on others], it will be measured back to you.

Matthew 6:20-21- But gather and heap up and store for yourselves treasures in heaven, where neither moth nor rust nor worm consume and destroy, and where thieves do not break through and steal; 21 For where your treasure is, there will your heart be also.

Press through. For all that seems to be coming apart so much more am I holding together. I will never leave you nor forsake you. Give and it will be given unto you. Pressed down shaken together pouring over. Sing praises in the midst of all you face. Stand in the face of adversity. You are the head and not the tail above only and not beneath. Give Me your burdens. Let Me bear the weight so that you continue to stand strong. Direction is coming. The answer is there. Wait with great expectancy. Peace I GIVE you My peace I leave with you. I am strong. I am your strength. You will mount up as eagles.

SEEK

Hebrews 13:5 Father God, help me to let my character or moral disposition be free from love of money [including greed, avarice, lust, and craving for earthly possessions] and be satisfied with my present [circumstances and with what I have]; for You [God] Yourself has said, You will not in any way fail me nor give me up nor leave me without support. [You will] not, [You will] not, [You will] not in any degree leave me helpless nor forsake nor let [me] down (relax Your hold on me)! [Assuredly not!]

Continue your prayer here, keep it scriptural

_____
_____
_____
_____
_____

_____
_____
_____

In Jesus name, Amen (in the authority of Jesus, so be it in my life)

People you are praying for

_____
_____
_____
_____
_____

SPEAK

Declare this over yourself, stand on the Word of God Matthew 6:24-No one can serve two masters; for either he will hate the one and love the other or he will stand by and be devoted to the one and despise and be against the other. You cannot serve God and mammon (deceitful riches, money, possessions, or whatever is trusted in).

LISTEN

Read and meditate on these verses this week Matthew 6:19-34 Teaching about Money and Possessions.

HEAR

What revelation, wisdom and understanding did you gain this week?

_____
_____
_____
_____

DO

How is God moving you? How did you apply His guidance to your life this week? How do you see God transforming you?

_____
_____
_____
_____

BE ENCOURAGED

Malachi 3:10- Bring all tithes (the whole tenth of your income into the storehouse, that there may be food in My house, and prove Me now by it, of hosts, if I will not open the windows of heaven for you and pour out a blessing, that there shall not be room enough to receive it.

CLARITY

It is like most things in the kingdom of God. The principle of giving and receiving is the complete opposite from how the world views it. Either it's every man for himself, or there is always a return expected in some form. Even if it is recognition or shame built in with what you've received from the other party. God is the opposite. For God so LOVED the world He GAVE. He didn't give because He expected anything in return for Himself. He gave BECAUSE He loved. That was it. End of story. Jesus came and took back what man had freely given away that was never intended to be Satan's. When man gave to Satan their authority and dominion, they didn't realize what they were doing. They gave away their own free will. They gave away the right to choose life or death. But because Jesus came, He reclaimed our salvation, our eternity, our free will to choose Whom we will serve (Joshua 24:15). Well, if we choose to serve the Lord, He was willing to come and serve us and die for us. Why do we not long to give the Lord every part of us including our tithe of money, time, and talent's. It's a heart thing. We need to be transformed in our hearts to LONG to give to the Lord that in our obedience, He may pour out blessings that cannot be contained but our heart should be that God can use those blessings to bless others as ourselves. Not just to look for a return on our giving.

TESTIMONY

Tithing isn't just about writing a check every month or putting an extra five in for special donations. Of course those things are important, but your heart will lead you in other ways that you can tithe. It's about giving in all areas. As I began to grow in the Lord, I wanted to become involved in the church. I wasn't really mature enough in the Lord to jump right in and begin leading classes, but I longed to be used. So, I started where I was at and asked God to put on my heart where I can be used. He led me to sign up to help in our elementary ministry checking kids in before service. I knew I still needed to be fed so it was perfect for me. Once a week I would make sure all the kids were checked in safely and then I would go into service myself. I didn't realize until later that this was a form of tithing. God positioned me there so that He could use me to help their service run smoothly. The service I was providing each week was needed and ministered to others. I stuck with it, continued to grow and make friends. As I stayed faithful, the time came that they needed help within the service. They were looking for guest speakers to come in, write and deliver a message. The door opened for me to be stretched and to be used further. It wasn't because I was trying to achieve something, it was simply because I was being obedient and faithful to where I was that I was able to be used to be a blessing to others and grow in my walk. Doing things I had never known I would be able to do. When we give of our time and talents, we are doing kingdom work and God is using us. When He sees we are faithful in one thing, He will trust us with more. Because, our heart is in giving to and for others.

YOUR PERSONAL TESTIMONY

_____
_____
_____
_____
_____
_____
_____
_____

WEEK 37 MATURING

1 Corinthians 2:6 Yet when we are among the full-grown (spiritually mature Christians who are ripe in understanding) we do impart a [higher] wisdom (the knowledge of the divine plan previously hidden); but it is indeed not a wisdom of this present age or of this world nor of the leaders and rulers of this age, who are being brought to nothing and are doomed to pass away.

Lord, where have You taken me?
I have taken you one step closer.
Lord, why did you draw me here?
I draw you out from your ways and into mine.

SEEK

Ephesians 4:14-15 Father, I declare that I may no longer be a child, tossed [like a ship] to and fro between chance gusts of teaching and wavering with every changing wind of doctrine, [the prey of] the cunning cleverness of unscrupulous men, [gamblers engaged] in every shifting form of trickery in inventing errors to mislead. Rather, let my life lovingly express truth [in all things, speaking truly, dealing truly, living truly]. Enfolded in love, let me grow up in every way and in all things into You Who is the Head, [even] Christ (the Messiah the Anointed One).

(Continue your prayer here, keep it scriptural)

_____
_____
_____
_____
_____
_____
_____
_____

in Jesus name, Amen (in the authority of Jesus, so be it in my life)

People you are praying for

_____
_____
_____

_____

_____

SPEAK

Declare this over yourself, stand on the Word of God
1 Corinthians 1:25 [This is] because the foolish thing [that has its source in] God is wiser than men, and the weak thing [that springs] from God is stronger than men.

LISTEN

Read and meditate on these verses this week 1 Corinthians 1:18-31 The Wisdom of God

HEAR

What revelation, wisdom, and understanding did you gain this week?

_____

_____

_____

_____

_____

DO

How is God moving you? How did you apply His guidance to your life this week? How do you see God transforming you?

_____

_____

_____

_____

_____

BE ENCOURAGED

Colossians 2:2-3 [For my concern is] that their hearts may be braced (comforted, cheered, and encouraged) as they are knit together in love, that they may come to have all the abounding wealth and blessings of assured conviction of understanding, and that they may become progressively more intimately acquainted with and may know more definitely and accurately and thoroughly that mystic secret of God, [which is] Christ (the

Anointed One). In Him all the treasures of [divine] wisdom (comprehensive insight into the ways and purposes of God) and [all the riches of spiritual] knowledge and enlightenment are stored up and lie hidden.

CLARITY

We don't always see what God sees, but He continues to reveal His ways to us. The more we seek Him, the more we find Him. The more we seek Him before we step, the more we are able to be led By Him. His ways are very different from how we would do things in our own strength. The way God shows us to do things will always glorify Him. We look back after all is said and done and we see God in it, we see the testimony He has given us. He equips us with the power of His blood and the words of our testimonies. In our weakest moments, He is glorified.

TESTIMONY

I found myself in a situation with someone, where we just didn't see eye to eye. I could see where their struggle was, and even had much that I could say about what they should be doing to fix some things. Nothing was working, so when I finally went to God about me, I asked Him to speak to me about MY heart. I asked Him to show me where I was missing it and to help me change MY heart. In this time, I became super aware of my attitude and words. I recognized how no matter whether I was right or wrong about the situation, nothing was going to get better until I let God get a hold of me. Once I allowed God to take the lead and deal with me, I was able to have a different perspective and the relationship healed. The situation got better and I stopped trying to correct the other person. They were able to receive love as my heart changed toward them. I never had to tell them what was different. In the spiritual, there was a shift and we responded to it. The world does not handle situations this way, instead the world responds with emotions and emotions react. Reactions usually are not healing by bring division. God's ways brings unity and love into our lives and the circumstances we face.

YOUR PERSONAL TESTIMONY

_____
_____

WEEK 38 BREAD OF LIFE

John 6:50-51 But this is the Bread that comes down out of heaven, so that one may eat of it and not die. I am the Living Bread that came down out of heaven. If anyone eats of this Bread [believes in Me, accepts Me as Savior], he will live forever. And the Bread thatI will give for the life of the world is My flesh (body)."

The mind is the battlefield of the soul. Be careful what you feed on. Just because food is in front of you doesn't mean it's good for you and that you should eat it. Study it, know what's in it. What does it contain? Food may look good but be full of poisons, some will kill you instantly, others slowly, but all poisons lead to the same road.

SEEK

Isaiah 55:2 Father God, I speak to mountains in my life, desiring to spend my money on that which is bread, And my earnings for what does satisfy. I am listening carefully to You Lord, and I desire to eat what is good, and to let my soul delight in abundance.

Continue your prayer here, keep it scriptural

_____
_____
_____
_____
_____
_____
_____
_____

In Jesus name, Amen (In the authority of Jesus, so be it in my life)

People you are praying for

_____
_____
_____
_____
_____

SPEAK

Declare this over yourself, stand on the Word of God John 6:35 Jesus replied to them, "I am the Bread of Life. The one who comes to Me will never be hungry, and the one who believes in Me [as Savior] will never be thirsty [for that one will be sustained spiritually].

LISTEN

Read these verses and meditate on them this week John 6:25-59 Jesus the Bread of Life

HEAR

What revelation, wisdom and understanding did you gain this week?

_____
_____
_____
_____
_____

DO

How is God moving you? How did you apply His guidance to your life this week? How do you see God transforming you?

_____
_____
_____
_____
_____

BE ENCOURAGED

Revelation 2:7- He who has an ear, let him hear and heed what the Spirit says to the churches. To him who overcomes [the world through believing that Jesus is the Son of God], I will grant [the privilege] to eat [the fruit] from the tree of life, which is in the Paradise of God.'

CLARITY

Jesus is the Bread of Life. John 1:1 tells us that, (In the beginning [before all time] was the Word (Christ), and the Word was with God, and the Word was God Himself). When we eat the Bread of Life, we are eating the Word, we are eating Jesus. In the sense that we are taking in God Himself, letting Him reveal more Truth to us and filling ourselves up with Life. In this process, we are renewing our minds and being transformed. Our flesh is dying more and more. The true creation God made us to be is being brought out in us more and more. Which who we are is truly the image of God. We just need to feed on the right things and let the nutrients of the Word or the Bread, grow us.

TESTIMONY

I used to be very quiet and shy. I was always the girl who would sit back in a room and let everyone visit. I always managed to find a way to blend in with the plants so to speak. I came to a point where I was tired of living life this way. I was reminded of the scripture Prov. 18:24 (KJV) A man that hath friends must shew himself friendly: and there is a friend that sticketh closer than a brother. I began small, smiling more, saying hello more. Then I began just stepping out in faith and having small conversations. But it wasn't until the man I call my spiritual father said something that stuck with me. He said that he asked Holy Spirit to show him who needed ministering to and then he would go over and let God use him. This grabbed hold of my heart because I just had compassion for those who needed encouragement and freedom in an area. I began doing this and amazing things began happening. It was no longer about me seeking friends, but me seeking God as He led. As He used me to minister to others, I became closer and closer friends with Him. In this He filled me, I no longer felt a void. I also grew out of my shyness. Now, those who know me can't believe I was ever the quiet girl. As I sought God, He transformed me. He brought life to a branch of my life that was producing no fruit.

YOUR PERSONAL TESTIMONY

_____
_____
_____

WEEK 39 DISCIPLE

Joshua 24:14-15- Now therefore, [reverently] fear the Lord and serve Him in sincerity and in truth; put away the gods which your fathers served on the other side of the [Euphrates] River and in Egypt, and serve the Lord. 15 And if it seems evil to you to serve the Lord, choose for yourselves this day whom you will serve, whether the gods which your fathers served on the other side of the River, or the gods of the Amorites, in whose land you dwell; but as for me and my house, we will serve the Lord.

I have not left you. I have not forsaken you. I am your Father who loves you. Walk in your position as My child. You are royalty. You are a child of the Most High God. The keys to the kingdom are yours. The only one who can keep you down is you. Stand taller than ever before. Walk straighter than ever before. Keep My commandments that all may be well with you. It may be simple but it isn't easy. Salvation is free, but it's the cost of living in freedom that is high. Am I worth it to you? You were worth it to Me from the very beginning. Keep your eyes on the prize. Run your race.

SEEK

Mark 16:17-18 Father, I thank You that because I believe and I am Your child, these attesting signs will accompany me who believes: in Your name I will drive out demons; I will speak in new languages; I will pick up serpents; and [even] if I drink anything deadly, it will not hurt me; I will lay my hands on the sick, and they will get better.

Continue your prayer here, keep it scriptural

_____
_____
_____
_____
_____
_____
_____

in Jesus name, Amen (in the authority of Jesus, so be it in my life)

People you are praying for-

_____
_____
_____
_____
_____

SPEAK

Declare this over yourself, stand on the Word of God Isaiah 53:5 But He was wounded for our transgressions, He was bruised for our guilt and iniquities; the chastisement [needful to obtain] peace and well-being for us was upon Him, and with the stripes [that wounded] Him we are healed and made whole.

LISTEN

Read and meditate on these verses this week Isaiah 52:13-53:12 The LORD'S Suffering Servant

HEAR

What revelation, wisdom and understanding did you gain this week?

_____
_____
_____
_____
_____

DO-How is God moving you? How did you apply His guidance to your life this week? How do you see God transforming you?

_____
_____
_____
_____
_____

BE ENCOURAGED

Ephesians 2:8 For it is by free grace (God's unmerited favor) that you are saved (delivered from judgment and made partakers of Christ's salvation) through [your] faith. And this [salvation] is not of yourselves [of your own doing, it came not through your own striving], but it is the gift of God;

CLARITY

As children of the Most High God, we freely enjoy His salvation. It is a free gift that He gives with no strings. Discipleship comes at a greater cost which requires His mercy and grace in our lives in order to grow in it. We are called to keep His commandments which are all fulfilled in love. This is a tougher road than it sounds like. When we are willing to say yes Lord, it isn't because we in and of ourselves are ready or capable of achieving great things. It is because we are willing to submit and humble ourselves enough to see our flaws and have confidence in the Lord that He equips us and strengthens us to accomplish what He has called us to do. It is all for God's glory. We are His children and we are royalty in His kingdom, but it isn't so that we may boast, but so that we may love.

TESTIMONY

I began going to church. I gave my life to the Lord. I was saved. I was set free. Praise God. Then I hungered for more. I didn't know fully what I was asking for, but the journey began when my heart desired to be a disciple of Jesus, not just saved by grace through faith.I wanted to put into action what I had just received. I began studying and couldn't get enough. I took classes and couldn't get enough. I joined groups and yet, I was still hungry. I knew there was still more. Then, God began using in leadership roles, and what God showed me immediately through amazing examples of leaders that I was blessed to learn from, was that leadership is never about you.

It is always about the people. It is about serving them, meeting their needs, and giving of yourself. As soon as I thought God had me right where I was supposed to be, more hunger rumbled in my spirit. God is always preparing us for the next step. He will always have a purpose for us. Salvation is enough for us to gain entry into heaven, but it's in our relationship that we build with the Lord that we experience His glory and heaven here on earth.

YOUR PERSONAL TESTIMONY

_____

_____

_____

_____

_____

WEEK 40 FAMILY

Hebrews 10:24-25 and let us consider [thoughtfully] how we may encourage one another to love and to do good deeds, not forsaking our meeting together [as believers for worship and instruction], as is the habit of some, but encouraging one another; and all the more [faithfully] as you see the day [of Christ's return] approaching.

We are not all called to be Pastors. But we are all called to love. We are not all called to the same office but we are called to go into the world and share the Good News. Although we are not all called to the same office, we are called to a church family so that we may pray for and lift up each other. We each only have a certain amount of perspective. It isn't until we have walked in someone else's shoes that we can share a portion of their perspective. When God lets you gain a small amount of someone else's view, praise Him in it and pray for them. We never truly know the weight someone else bears. This is why we are to love and not judge. Only God truly knows. When God calls you to a specific church family, remember He has called you to just that. A portion of His entire family, to do your part, to stand firm with your family and not to walk away leaving it and yourself incomplete.

SEEK

Romans 12:10-13 Father God, I declare today that I will be devoted to one another with [authentic] brotherly affection [as a member of one family], give preference to one another in honor; never lagging behind in diligence; aglow in the Spirit, enthusiastically serving You Lord; constantly rejoicing in hope [because of our confidence in Christ], steadfast and patient in distress, devoted to prayer [continually seeking wisdom, guidance, and strength], contributing to the needs of Your people, pursuing [the practice of] hospitality.

Continue your prayer here, keep it scriptural

_____
_____
_____
_____
_____
_____

in Jesus name, Amen (in the authority of Jesus, so be it in my life)

People you are praying for

_____
_____
_____
_____
_____

SPEAK

Declare this over yourself, stand on the Word of God Colossians 3:15 Let the peace of Christ [the inner calm of one who walks daily with Him] be the controlling factor in your hearts [deciding and settling questions that arise]. To this peace indeed you were called as members in one body [of believers]. And be thankful [to God always].

LISTEN

Read and meditate on these verses this week Colossians 3:1-17 Living the New Life

HEAR

What revelation, wisdom and understanding did you gain this week?

_____
_____
_____
_____
_____

DO

How is God moving you? How did you apply His guidance to your life this week? How do you see God transforming you?

_____
_____
_____

BE ENCOURAGED

Exodus 17:12- But Moses' hands were heavy and grew weary. So [the other men] took a stone and put it under him and he sat on it. Then Aaron and Hur held up his hands, one on one side and one on the other side; so his hands were steady until the going down of the sun.

CLARITY

So often the body of Christ loves to get caught up in who's right and who's wrong. We shift our focus off of what we've been called to do. LOVE! That is it. The next time someone wants to voice their opinion about how wonderful their church is and they want to know why you go to your church, simply share this message. That is the church family God has planted me with. For all the wonderful reasons and the not so wonderful reasons. God has put me there to love my brothers and sisters in the Lord and who am I to argue with God? I know my family isn't perfect, but they are my family. As I would never disown the family I was born into, I would never disown the family I was called to. They are a part of my spiritual DNA and they are part of who I am in Christ. This is how we should see our church. Not as a place to go until we get mad about something or it becomes inconvenient, but a place where we all need each other, period. In the beauty and in the mess.

TESTIMONY

The very first time I experienced a true sense of family within the church, was when we first began attending our church family and a greater by the name of Jerry, sought me and my children out each Sunday morning in the lobby to see how we were doing and to find out what I needed prayer for. Then he would always encourage me. It broke my heart when he passed, but it truly impacted me in a way that I will never forget and that kind of love has been forever ingrained in my spiritual DNA.

YOUR PERSONAL TESTIMONY

_____

_____

_____

_____

_____

_____

_____

_____

WEEK 41 CLARITY

John 14:27 Peace I leave with you; My [own] peace I now give and bequeath to you. Not as the world gives do I give to you. Do not let your hearts be troubled, neither let them be afraid. [Stop allowing yourselves to be agitated and disturbed; and do not permit yourselves to be fearful and intimidated and cowardly and unsettled.]

The greater the storm, the greater the testimony. Take your eyes off the wind and the rain. Keep them stayed on Me. Do not doubt in your heart and walk on the deeper waters. I pull you up when you cry out. Winds change, rain stops, but I am the same always and I will never leave you nor forsake you. No storm is bigger than Me. Storms do not quiet Me, I quiet the storms!

SEEK

John 14:27 Father God, I thank You that Peace You leave with me; Your [perfect] peace You give to me; not as the world gives do You give to me. I will not let my heart be troubled, nor will I let it be afraid. [I will let Your perfect peace calm me in every circumstance and give me courage and strength for every challenge.] In Jesus name, Amen (in the authority of Jesus, so be it in my life)

Continue your prayer here, keep it scriptural

_____
_____
_____
_____
_____
_____
_____
_____

People you are praying for

_____
_____
_____
_____
_____

SPEAK

Declare this over yourself, stand on the Word of God 1 Corinthians 13:12-13 For now [in this time of imperfection] we see in a mirror dimly [a blurred reflection, a riddle, an enigma], but then [when the time of perfection comes we will see reality] face to face. Now I know in part [just in fragments], but then I will know fully, just as I have been fully known [by God]. And now there remain: faith [abiding trust in God and His promises], hope [confident expectation of external salvation], love [unselfish love for others growing out of God's love for me], these three [the choicest graces]; but the greatest of these is love.

LISTEN

Read and meditate on these verses this week, 1 Corinthians 13:1-13 Love is the Greatest

HEAR

What revelation, wisdom and understanding did you gain this week?

_____
_____
_____
_____
_____

DO

How is God moving you? How did you apply His guidance to your life this week? How do you see God transforming you?

_____
_____
_____
_____
_____

BE ENCOURAGED

Matthew 14:27 But immediately He spoke to them, saying, "Take courage, it is I! Do not be afraid!"

CLARITY

In the midst of the storms and trials that we all face in life, there is always clarity when we remember what to focus on. Love is the greatest power in the midst of everything. Love always overcomes. Remember to stay focused on that. Peace keeps the loud screaming circumstances quieted as we seek the Lord for guidance in our days. When we focus on God, love and peace become the strength that God gives us to draw from and as we walk the path God gives us to go, we gain clarity as we see that He is bigger than anything we will ever face.

TESTIMONY

As a homeschooling mom, many of my testimonies will circle around that. However, what could be more powerful than being called to train my children up in the way they should go. That being said, so many days are filled with me having to refocus on God because I do not have clarity as to why He has called me to do this. Then suddenly, as I turn to God, choose to bring out the love and peace He has so graciously filled me with, that moment comes. I begin to see the fruit of what being able to spend time and be an influence to my children is doing in their lives. One is desiring to walk with me and hug me while I'm in my prayer time and then their prayer life begins to mature. Another begins to write worship songs. Yet another, shows such a heart of compassion toward others in such a powerful way. They don't yet fully realize the gifting's that are being matured in their lives, but God is faithful and this clarity keeps me strong and moving forward in what He has called me to do for my children.

YOUR PERSONAL TESTIMONY

_____
_____
_____
_____
_____
_____
_____
_____

WEEK 42 RELATIONSHIP

John 1:10-13 He (Christ) was in the world, and though the world was made through Him, the world did not recognize Him. He came to that which was His own [that which belonged to Him- His world, His creation, His possession], and those who were His own [people- the Jewish nation] did not receive and welcome Him. But to as many as did receive and welcome Him, He gave the right [the authority, the privilege] to become children of God, that is, to those who believe in (adhere to, trust in, and rely on) His name- who were born, not of blood [natural conception], nor of the will of the flesh [physical impulse], nor of the will of man [that of a natural father], but of God [that is, a divine and supernatural birth- they are born of God- spiritually transformed, renewed, sanctified].

I desire to walk and talk with you. I know you, but do you know Me? I long for you to turn to Me in the big and small, the loud and the quiet, the happy and the sad times. I know your heart, I long for you to know Mine. I ache for you to open up to Me and let Me in that you may hear Me when I speak and that you have the desire to come to Me in every circumstance. Talk to Me, listen to Me, as we walk things out together. See hear and know greater truths and you grow an intimate relationship with Me.

SEEK

John 15:5 Father, You are the vine; I am the branch. As I remain in You and You in me I bear much fruit, for [otherwise] apart from You [that is, cut off from vital union with You] I can do nothing. Continue your prayer here, keep it scriptural

_____

_____

_____

_____

_____

_____

_____

in Jesus name, Amen (in the authority of Jesus, so be it in my life)

People you are praying for

_____
_____
_____
_____
_____

SPEAK

Declare this over yourself, stand on the Word of God John 16:7- However, I am telling you nothing but the truth when I say it is profitable (good, expedient, advantageous) for you that I go away. because if I do not go away, the Comforter (Counselor, Helper, Advocate, Intercessor, Strengthener, Standby) will not come to you [into close fellowship with you]; but if I go away, I will send Him to you [to be in close fellowship with you].

LISTEN

Read and meditate on these verses this week John 16:5-15
The Work of the Holy Spirit

HEAR

What revelation, wisdom and understanding did you gain this week?

_____
_____
_____
_____
_____

DO

How is God moving you? How did you apply His guidance to your life this week? How do you see God transforming you?

_____
_____
_____
_____
_____

BE ENCOURAGED

Philippians 2:13 For it is [not your strength, but it is] God who is effectively at work in you, both to will and to work [that is, strengthening, energizing, and creating in you the longing and the ability to fulfill your purpose] for His good pleasure.

CLARITY

Prayer isn't a formula, it is a conversation with our God who loves us so dearly. Have a heart to heart with Him. Be respectful, but be honest. Speak from your heart and remember it is so crucial to let Him speak to you as well. He will share wonderful things with you in your time with Him. he will remind you of how much He loves you. He will give you guidance in your life. He will ask you to do things for Him. he will encourage you, and convict you with love when it is necessary. That is what our good Daddy does and it is always with love that He speaks to us. He will plant seeds and sometimes we will need to be patient. Trust that He knows what He is doing and that His timing is perfect. Prayer builds our relationship with Him. This is our Daddy time. remember you can speak to Him anytime, anywhere. He is always available for you. It doesn't always need to be a long conversation, but He desires for you to want His input even in things that seem small. Praise Him through things and thank Him for His goodness. remember He loves you and knows your heart. There are many ways to pray, but it is always a heart condition and God honors that. He loves to hear our heart even when we are hurting or don't even have the words. Pray in the Spirit and experience the power of letting Holy Spirit pray through you the perfect will of God. Trust that as you grow in your prayer life with Him that He will continue to speak to you. You will learn to recognize when He is speaking.

TESTIMONY

The revelation of what prayer really is, unlocked the door that I never knew even existed. I knew that prayer was important, but I didn't really know how to pray or even what it truly was. When I learned that God meets us where we're at and that He knows our heart, I wasn't afraid of being wrong in my prayer life anymore. Then when i understood how easy it truly is to converse WITH God, boy it was on. I just began speaking to

Him and trusting by faith that he would always have something to tell me. I got to a place in my prayer life, that I received the baptism of the Holy Spirit and as I grew in praying in tongues, I began receiving words or encouragement, words of knowledge, and God continues to grow me. It has nothing to do with me, it is not some major feat I have accomplished, it is all God and for His glory. I have a hunger and I have times where I have to push more than others, but as I continue to seek Him to use me, He does. I came to the understanding that God can use anyone for His plan and purpose. He is simply looking for an obedient heart that wants to be His hands and feet. This humbles me every day. To know that the God of all creation desires to talk with me and use me in His great plan. It continues to remind me how small I am and yet how much I matter to Him as we all do. He is truly our perfect Father.

YOUR PERSONAL TESTIMONY

_____
_____
_____
_____
_____
_____
_____
_____

WEEK 43 STAND

COLOSSIANS 1:23 [and He will do this] if you continue in the faith, well-grounded and steadfast, and not shifting away from the [confident] hope [that is a result] of the gospel that you have heard, which was proclaimed in all creation under heaven, and of which [gospel] I, Paul, was made a minister.

Just watch and see what I am about to do. Stand strong in your faith. Know who you stand with. HAHA! no fear, no doubt. My love abounds and peace strengthens you. Be still in your boldness. I say speak to your mountains and watch what happens, HA! I am the Lord God. Just trust Me.

SEEK

1 Corinthians 15:58 Father, I declare that I am steadfast, immovable, always excelling in the work of the Lord [always doing my best and doing more than is needed], being continually aware that my labor [even to the point of exhaustion] in the Lord is not futile nor wasted [it is never without purpose]. Continue your prayer here, keep it scriptural

_____
_____
_____
_____
_____
_____
_____
_____

in Jesus name, Amen (in the authority of Jesus, so be it in my life)

People you are praying for

_____
_____
_____
_____
_____

SPEAK

Declare this over yourself, stand on the Word of God

Hebrews 10:23 Let us seize and hold tightly the confession of our hope without wavering, for He who promised is reliable and trustworthy and faithful [to His word];

LISTEN

Read and meditate on these verses this week Hebrews 10:19-39 A Call to Persevere

HEAR

What revelation, wisdom and understanding did you gain this week?

_____
_____
_____
_____
_____

DO

How is God moving you? How did you apply His guidance to your life this week? How do you see God transforming you?

_____
_____
_____
_____
_____

BE ENCOURAGED

1 Peter 5:9 But resist him, be firm in your faith [against his attack- rooted, established, immovable], knowing that the same experiences of suffering are being experienced by your brothers and sisters throughout the world. [You do not suffer alone.]

CLARITY

As we confess Jesus as our Lord, we are not just receiving His salvation, but we are confessing that He is our boss. Which means we believe what He says, we will not let anything sway us from that. We will continue to believe Him above the circumstances. Even in the darkest times, it is our place to say

NO! The Word of God is my final authority above and beyond anything that comes my way. Because My God is the same God that delivered His people out of Egypt. the same God who saved the three men from inside the firy furnace, and the same God who died on the cross for me and delivered me from myself. I WILL NOT BE MOVED!

TESTIMONY

I never realized how much doubt and fear I had in my life until I made Jesus my final authority. I used to speak so much doubt and fear over myself and my life that it's no wonder things were going the direction they were. As my mind is renewed and I am continually being transformed, I am learning how to declare and believe more and more what the Word says over what things look like. However, there are always people around me that don't have that same renewed understanding. I used to just quietly let them say what they wanted to and say that I was believing what I wanted. I began to realize that I was still allowing fear and unbelief to be spoken into MY life. So, I began kindly telling people that I am only believing in this and that I need those around me to believe the same way. That looking at things in a bleak manner isn't going to do me any good. I need to be surrounded by those who will believe the same way. It isn't always easy, but being bold even with family who maybe doesn't get it shows an example of strength they may have never been exposed to before. I have had to endure through a period of time and truly stand on what I have said I'm believing even if it looks to everyone else like a mess. When it is all said and done, God is always faithful and has always backed whatever I have proclaimed according to His Word. Life always brings forth life. The Word is living.

YOUR PERSONAL TESTIMONY-

_____
_____
_____
_____
_____
_____
_____
_____

WEEK 44 LEAST IS GREATEST

Matthew 19:30 But many who are first [in this world] will be last [in the world to come]; and the last, first.

Do not put God in the box we hold. It is too small to contain Him. If God were limited to our thoughts, He would be a limited God. But thank You Jesus, His thoughts are not our thoughts, His ways are not our ways. He can and will do exceeding and abundantly above all we can ask or think. He makes all things new. For how big is our God, that we can cast all our cares upon Him and He can bear them. We serve a God big enough that He made Himself a servant, and in that His love is limitless. Only a great King makes Himself the least important in order to save His people. Our God is not only King, He is Abba Father with boundless love, He is our provider who gives. Our restorer who returns what is lost. He dwells in us, walks with us, is everywhere at the same time. How great is our God! He is limitless.

SEEK

Hebrews 10:24 Father, help me to consider [thoughtfully] how I may encourage others to love and to do good deeds. Continue your prayer here, keep it scriptural

_____
_____
_____
_____
_____
_____
_____
_____

in Jesus name, Amen (in the authority of Jesus, so be it in my life

People you are praying for

_____
_____
_____
_____

SPEAK

Declare this over yourself, stand on the Word of God John 13:12-14 So when He had washed their feet and put on His [outer] robe and reclined at the table again, He said to them, "Do you understand what I have done for you? You call Me teacher and Lord, and you are right in doing so, for that is who I am. So if I, the Lord and the Teacher, washed your feet, you ought to wash one another's feet as well.

LISTEN

Read and meditate on these verses this week John 13:1-17 Jesus Washes His Disciples' Feet

HEAR

What revelation, wisdom and understanding did you gain this week?

_____

_____

_____

_____

_____

DO

How is God moving you? How did you apply His guidance to your life this week? How do you see God transforming you?

_____

_____

_____

_____

_____

BE ENCOURAGED

Hebrews 6:10-12 For God is not unjust so as to forget your work and the love which you have shown for His name in ministering to [the needs of] the saints (God's people), as you do. And we desire for each one of you to show the same diligence [all the way through] so as to realize and enjoy the full assurance of hope until the end, so that you will not be [spiritually] sluggish, but [will instead be] imitators of those who through faith [lean on God with absolute trust and confidence in Him and in His power] and by patient endurance [even when suffering] are [now] inheriting the promises.

CLARITY

In the world, success is driven by and obtained by the flesh. As the flesh lusts for itself, it is clear that someone who obtains greatness in the flesh will lift himself up as others are under him. In God's kingdom, it is the exact opposite. Jesus demonstrated this to us in many ways. But as I mentioned before, the washing of the feet was one way, but the major ways were, that He came into this world as a baby, He was not born into royalty, but rather He was born in a manger. He spent His life teaching, healing, and doing for others. Then He died on the cross for us. Yet, He is the King of Kings and the Lord of Lords. He is the great I Am. So, when we focus on what we can do for others, we need to remember the more we lower ourselves, the more useful we are for the Lord toward others.

TESTIMONY

Now, financially I was not well off. I would receive help from others and this was truly humbling. I always wanted to be the person to give though. I heard it said that God will use what you have and that opened my eyes to a new understanding. So, one year our church was having a guest speaker. They needed volunteers to help with things during and such. Well, with my children and other commitments I didn't have much available time. I really wanted to help. Then I saw that they needed someone to pick up the parking lot. I thought, I can do that. So, my youngest daughter and I set out early in the morning before Bible Study and we went up and down the rows picking up papers and all kinds of fun things that were laying around out there. It was cool and windy. It even began raining at one point.

Together we stuck it out and got the job done. We had fun because my heart was happy to be of help. My daughter was happy because she saw my example and in turn wanted to be a help as well. I didn't realize anyone had even noticed, but later multiple people had encouraged us with kind words of how nice the lot looked. It wasn't the compliments that filled my heart. It was knowing that I was usable and able to provide a need for someone else no matter the task. God needs us all to be willing to step in even when the job isn't glamorous.

YOUR PERSONAL TESTIMONY

_____

_____

_____

_____

_____

_____

_____

_____

WEEK 45 SING

Ephesians 2:10 For we are His workmanship [His own master work, a work of art], created in Christ Jesus [reborn from above- spiritually transformed, renewed, ready to be used] for good works, which God prepared [for us] beforehand [taking paths which He set], so that we would walk in them [living the good life which He prearranged and made ready for us].

When the wind comes, I will fill your sails and the instrument I made you to be will make a beautiful sound that will glorify Me.

SEEK

Isaiah 10:15 Father God, as I may be the ax I am not able to lift myself over You who chops with me. As I may be the saw I am not able to magnify myself over You who wields me. Father, that would be like a club moving You who lifts me, or like a staff raising myself who is not [made of] wood [like itself]!

Continue your prayer here, keep it scriptural-

_____
_____
_____
_____
_____
_____
_____
_____

in Jesus name, Amen (in the authority of Jesus, so be it in my life)

People you are praying for

_____
_____
_____
_____
_____

SPEAK

Declare this over yourself, stand on the Word of God

Romans 6:13- Do not continue offering or yielding your bodily members [and faculties] to sin as instruments (tools) of wickedness. But offer and yield yourselves to God as though you have been raised from the dead to [perpetual] life, and your bodily members [and faculties] to God, presenting them as implements of righteousness,

Matthew 9:36-38 When He saw the throngs, He was moved with pity and sympathy for them, because they were bewildered (harassed and distressed and dejected and helpless), like sheep without a shepherd. 37 Then He said to His disciples, the harvest is indeed plentiful, but the laborers are few. 38 So pray to the Lord of the harvest to force out and thrust laborers into His harvest.

LISTEN

Read and meditate on these verses this week Romans 6, Matthew 9:35-38

HEAR

What revelation, wisdom and understanding did you gain this week?

_____
_____
_____
_____
_____

DO

How is God moving you? How did you apply His guidance in your life this week? How do you see God transforming you?

_____
_____
_____
_____
_____

BE ENCOURAGED

John 14:12-13 I assure you, most solemnly I tell you, if anyone steadfastly believes in Me, he will himself be able to do the things that I do; and he will do even greater things than these, because I go to the Father. 13 And I will do [I Myself will grant] whatever you ask in My Name [as presenting all that I AM], so that the Father may be glorified and extolled in (through) the Son.

CLARITY

As we are God's instruments, we are here to be used for Him and His glory. Not that we may "toot our own horn". Although He is faithful to reward us because He loves us, we are not truly worthy of it. We are merely here to do as He asks. We are here to be just what He has made us to be. He makes beautiful music with us when He uses us, but as we sing praises, they should only ever be of Him. God is good all the time. We are human. It is because of Jesus that we are made righteous in Him, not because of anything we have or will ever do.

TESTIMONY

As a child I was very unsure of myself. Compliments were few and far between. I never knew how to take them when they came my way. I came to the point where if someone complimented me I didn't really believe them anyway so I would just politely say thank you and keep going. As I have grown in my walk with the Lord, He has drawn a lot out of me that I never knew was there. I began receiving a lot of compliments and it felt very odd to me. It was scary and hard to know how to process them. I would quietly smile and keep going. I find I still do that at times. However, I have learned that compliments that are given to me are truly being given to the Lord. Although people thank me, it is really God who deserves all the glory and praise. So I kindly say thank you and then give God all the praise. It is truly just Him working through me. It is not me doing anything in my own strength. I have learned the hard way. Me doing things my way usually end up messy. So, I know it is all God. I'm just thankful to be used. As we sing praises we need to remember that truly everything is God's He just loves us enough to reward us with everything we need in every sense of the word. He is just that wonderful.

YOUR PERSONAL TESTIMONY

_____

_____

_____

_____

_____

_____

_____

_____

WEEK 46 TRUTH

Hebrews 4:12-For the Word that God speaks is alive and full of power [making it active, operative, energizing, and effective]; it is sharper than any two-edged sword, penetrating to the dividing line of the breath of life (soul) and [the immortal] spirit, and of joints and marrow [of the deepest parts of our nature], exposing and sifting and analyzing and judging the very thoughts and purposes of the heart.

My Truth is stronger
My Truth is bolder
My Truth breaks chains
My truth is pure love
My Truth is gentle
My Truth is kind
My Truth is comfort
My Love is Truth
I wrap you in My Truth
Love others in Truth
My blanket of Love is boundless- limitless
Speak to hearts from your heart as it lines up with Mine
Peace love and joy
Fill your lives with these as you fill your lives with Me
My truth is My Word I am the way the Truth and the Life
Speak life into your life.
Live the whole and prosperous life I have promised you.

SEEK

(2 Corinthians 4:4) Father God, my heart aches for those who do not see.{ among them the god of this world [Satan] has blinded the minds of the unbelieving to prevent them from seeing the illuminating light of the gospel of the glory of Christ, who is the image of God.} Father open their eyes that they may see, their ears that they may hear and soften their hearts that they may receive Your truth and your salvation.

Continue your prayer here, keep it scriptural

_____
_____
_____
_____
_____

in Jesus name, Amen (in the authority of Jesus, so be it in my life)

People you are praying for

_____

_____

_____

_____

_____

SPEAK

Declare this over yourself, stand on the Word of God Ephesians 4:23-24 and be continually renewed in the spirit of your mind [having a fresh, untarnished mental and spiritual attitude], and put on the new self [the regenerated and renewed nature], created in God's image, [godlike] in the righteousness and holiness of the truth [living in a way that expresses to God your gratitude for your salvation].

LISTEN

Read and meditate on these verses this week Ephesians 4:17-32 Living as Children of Light

HEAR

What revelation, wisdom and understanding did you gain this week?

_____

_____

_____

_____

_____

DO

How is God moving you? How did you apply His guidance to your life this week? How do you see God transforming you?

_____

_____

_____

_____

_____

BE ENCOURAGED

John 1:14 And the Word (Christ) became flesh, and lived among us; and we [actually] saw His glory, glory as belongs to the [One and] only begotten Son of the Father, [the Son who is truly unique, the only One of His kind, who is] full of grace and truth (absolutely free from deception).

CLARITY

Above and beyond what we know and understand according to the world, the Word is the Truth above all else. As we pray for those who don't yet see, we need to stand on what the Truth is and trust God that He always backs is Word.

TESTIMONY

I remember a lady who I was working closely with. When I first met her, she had a lot of weight from the world she was carrying with her. You could see it all over her. As I worked with her, prayed for her and asked God to reveal greater truths to her, I began to see a change. It wasn't over night, but it was in a matter of months which after the years the world spent beating her down, it was a quick work. I just remember the first time I saw pure joy on her face. She looked like an entirely different person. This didn't mean her life was now perfect, it meant that God was faithful and revealed greater truth and she received it. God's Truth transforms. He is a mighty God.

YOUR PERSONAL TESTIMONY

_____
_____
_____
_____
_____
_____
_____
_____

WEEK 47 DEFEATED FOE

2 Timothy 1:7 For God did not give us a spirit of timidity (of cowardice, of craven and cringing and fawning fear), but [He has given us a spirit] of power and of love and of a calm and well- balanced mind and discipline and self-control.

When you feel the fear try to come upon you, remember the authority I have given you. When fear tries to stop you from fulfilling a blessing I have promised you, remember the authority I have given you. It is never that fear won't come, it's that I have not given you this spirit and because fear comes from the god of this world, you are not required to pick it up and partner with it. Recognize the lie for what it is, renounce it and move forward in faith. Know that if fear is going to stop you from something good that I have for you, it is of the wrong spirit and you have full authority to tell it to go in My name. I am the Lord your God and everything you ever needed Me to do for you, was done at the cross.

SEEK

Galatians 2:20 Father, I thank You that I have been crucified with Christ [that is, in Him I have shared His crucifixion]; it is no longer I who live, but Christ lives in me. The life I now live in the body I live by faith [by adhering to, relying on, and completely trusting] in the Son of God, who loved me and gave Himself up for me.

Continue your Thanksgiving and praise here, keep it scriptural

_____
_____
_____
_____
_____
_____
_____
_____

in Jesus name, Amen (in the authority of Jesus, so be it in my life)

People you want to thank God for who were the laborers He used to draw you into salvation-

_____
_____
_____
_____
_____

SPEAK

Declare this over yourself, stand on the Word of God
1 Corinthians 15:57 but thanks be to God, who gives us the
victory [as conquerors] through our Lord Jesus Christ.

LISTEN

Read and meditate on these verses this week 1 Corinthians
15:35-58 The Resurrection Body

HEAR

What revelation, wisdom and understanding did you gain this
week?

_____
_____
_____
_____
_____

DO

How is God moving you? How did you apply His guidance to
your life this week? How do you see God transforming you?

_____
_____
_____
_____
_____

BE ENCOURAGED

Revelation 12:11 And they overcame and conquered him
because of the blood of the Lamb and because of the word of
their testimony, for they did not love their life and renounce
their faith even when faced with death.

CLARITY

Satan is defeated. Once and for all Jesus took back the authority that mankind willingly gave up to Satan. We still face trials and tribulations but we have the authority to overcome them, it's Jesus. As we learn to walk in that authority, we will see more victory in our lives. As the truth about fear is revealed, it won't have power in our lives like it once did. The lies of the enemy are a smoke screen. The less we believe the lies the more we believe the Truth. Speak life, speak truth, hold onto God's glory.

TESTIMONY

I had a child friend of one of my children ask me one time, "What if there were ghosts in your house?" This happened in a time where God had been revealing to me the authority I have over a defeated enemy. I politely looked him in the eye and said, "In Jesus name, they're not welcome in my home!" Now all the while thinking, wow normally that would've got my mind thinking on those things, but I had no doubt, no fear, no worry. I knew my God was bigger and there was nothing I needed to fear. That was the last time he ever brought anything like that up around me. Exercise your authority, it has the power you need in your life, Jesus has given it to us for a reason.

YOUR PERSONAL TESTIMONY

_____
_____
_____
_____
_____
_____
_____
_____
_____

WEEK 48 SPREAD

Mark 16:15- And He said to them, Go into all the world and preach and publish openly the good news (the Gospel) to every creature [of the whole human race].

The least of mine are the greatest. Do not pass someone by because they are not pleasant to be around. With compassion, share the love I have abundantly given you. That love will grow in you the more you give it away. Light spreads, love spreads, joy fills and overflows. In My name, be the salt and light spread My love and overflow in joy. Seek Me in prayer, but find Me in deed. Allow Me to show you Me in all that I ask you to do. Touch another heart and you touch Mine.

SEEK

Matthew 25:23 Father, my heart is that in my every day I look forward to the time when You say to me, Well done, you upright (honorable, admirable) and faithful servant! You have been faithful and trustworthy over a little; I will put you in charge of much. Enter into and share the joy (the delight, the blessedness) which your master enjoys. Until that day comes, my heart is to do as You have commanded, I will grow in going into all the world and preach and publish openly the good news (the gospel) to every creature [of the whole human race].

Continue your prayer here, keep it scriptural

_____
_____
_____
_____
_____
_____
_____
_____

in Jesus name, Amen (in the authority of Jesus, so be it in my life

People you are praying for that you have shared the gospel with

_____
_____
_____

_____

_____

SPEAK

Declare this over yourself, stand on the Word of God Matthew 25:40- And the King will reply to them, Truly I tell you, in so far as you did it for one of the least [in the estimation of men] of these My brethren, you did it for Me.

LISTEN

Read and meditate on these verses this week Matthew 25:31-46 The Final Judgement

HEAR

What revelation, wisdom and understanding did you gain this week?

_____

_____

_____

_____

_____

DO

How is God moving you? How did you apply His guidance to your life this week? How do you see God transforming you?

_____

_____

_____

_____

_____

BE ENCOURAGED

Hebrews 13:8 Jesus Christ is [eternally changeless, always] the same yesterday and today and forever.

CLARITY

No matter what else you do in life, the one thing we are all called to do is, share the good news. This does not mean beat people over the head with the Bible. This means love one another as we love our God and ourselves. When appropriate, share scripture. Jesus never forced anyone to receive what He had, but He never gave up that people would want what He had. We should be the very same way. Walk by example and when others show a hunger, share with them what you have. If God prompts you to pray for someone, do so with boldness and loving kindness. Speak life in the promises God has given us and remember that it is Jesus that is the power. We are the vessels He needs to be an impact to each other for Him.

TESTIMONY

I remember a time that I was new in the Lord, and a friend came to me in confidence. She had been making all kinds of choices that were damaging in her life. She broke down and shared everything with me. I never asked her to, she just did. God led me to give her Godly advice in certain areas and then I asked her about her relationship with the Lord. She told me it had been something she was thinking about lately. I was led to share a book with her. The next time I spoke with her, she had read the book, she began seeking the Lord and took my advice and her life was changing drastically for the better. God is able to do much when we are just willing to humble ourselves and be used. The love of Christ so often just looks like being a friend willing to take the time.

YOUR PERSONAL TESTIMONY

_____

_____

_____

_____

_____

_____

_____

_____

Made in the USA
Charleston, SC
02 June 2016